Can It Really Be Taught?

Can It Really Be Taught?
Resisting Lore in Creative Writing Pedagogy

Edited by

KELLY RITTER AND STEPHANIE VANDERSLICE

Boynton/Cook
HEINEMANN
Portsmouth, NH

Boynton/Cook Publishers, Inc.

361 Hanover Street
Portsmouth, NH 03801-3912
www.boyntoncook.com

Offices and agents throughout the world

© 2007 by Boynton/Cook Publishers, Inc.

Library of Congress Cataloging-in-Publication Data

Can it really be taught? : resisting lore in creative writing pedagogy /
[edited by] Kelly Ritter and Stephanie Vanderslice.
    p. cm.
  ISBN-13: 978-0-86709-588-3 (alk. paper)
  ISBN-10: 0-86709-588-1
  1. Creative writing (Higher education). 2. English
language—Rhetoric—Study and teaching (Higher). I. Ritter, Kelly. II.
Vanderslice, Stephanie.

PE1404.C327 2007
808'.0420711—dc22   2007000674

Editor: Charles I. Schuster
Production service: Aaron Downey, Matrix Productions Inc.
Production coordinator: Sonja S. Chapman
Cover design: Night & Day Design
Compositor: TechBooks
Manufacturing: Jamie Carter

Printed in the United States of America on acid-free paper
T & C Digital

For Wendy Bishop

Contents

Acknowledgments

Kelly wishes to thank her husband, Joshua Rosenberg, and her daughter, Sarah Rosenberg, for their love and support throughout the process of researching, writing, and editing this collection. She also thanks the College of Arts and Sciences and the Department of English at Southern Connecticut State University for providing the financial support and reassigned time necessary to bring this collection together, as well as her English department colleagues—in particular, Bob McEachern and Paul Petrie—who have continually appreciated, and supported, her interdisciplinary work in writing studies. She additionally thanks Jeanne Gunner and John Schilb at *College English* for publishing her other work on creative writing pedagogy and inspiring her to pursue this project, and her first poetry writing teacher, Karen Subach, who cared for Kelly's writing before (and after) anyone else would. Finally, Kelly thanks all of those creative writers who are committed to the highest quality teaching in our college and university classrooms, without whom none of this work would be possible.

Stephanie would like to express her appreciation to the University of Central Arkansas, whose ongoing support of her work has significantly expanded her scholarly reach. In addition, she must also thank her department chair, Dr. David Harvey, for a decade and counting in support and mentorship and for the freedom to pursue her academic interests. Along this vein, she is also grateful to her colleagues in the Department of Writing and Speech who individually and collectively contribute to a vibrant intellectual atmosphere where writing thrives at the center, and to the students there who bring joy to her daily work. Numerous mentors in composition and creative writing at the University of Louisiana at Lafayette also deserve mention, especially Dr. Jim MacDonald and Dr. Ann Dobie, who first introduced Stephanie to the intersections between creative writing and writing studies. A grateful nod also belongs to those who have been encouraging over many years and miles: Stephanie's family, especially her parents, grandparents, and late aunt, Elizabeth Muller, and long-time friends, Hannah Treitel Cosdon and Chris Motto. At last, always and everywhere, to her sons, Jackson and Wilson, and husband, John, belong Stephanie's deepest thanks.

Kelly and Stephanie also wish to jointly thank Charles Schuster at Heinemann Boynton/Cook for his patience and determination in shaping this book for publication, and for believing, first and foremost, that such a book was worthy of being read. We are forever grateful for his guidance.

Introduction

Creative Writing and the Persistence of "Lore" [1]

By Kelly Ritter and Stephanie Vanderslice

What's Lore Got to Do with It?

If you've ever been a student of creative writing in higher education, you may have recognized among your teachers certain profiles. There was the free-spirited graduate student who told you to explore your feelings and resisted giving grades or evaluations of any kind in favor of long conversations about the writing life, usually over tea and cookies. There was the seasoned professor who had a stellar reputation in the literary world, with numerous books and countless journal publications to his credit, who eschewed the university's trappings for an independent and efficient lifestyle outside of it. This translated to lots of time off campus, classes with a lot of stock lecturing and not much interaction, and interesting but minimal comments on student work. Then, there was the misunderstood professor, usually a famous writer herself, who was glamorous and worldly and espoused brilliant ideas about literature and culture but who bestowed varied attention on the many students in class. She had her favorite stars; others were ignored. To learn was to bask in her ethereal glow and to hope one day to be just like her.

All of these instructors are both real people and stereotypes. As in our previous work, we do not aim to point fingers at any one of them—or where they come from, or where they are going. But as you reflect on your time as a creative writing student, you may realize that these figures—writers who were given the honor of also being teachers—were your *role models*, instructors whose classrooms represented, for better or for worse, the way in which creative writing could be learned and taught. Most likely these instructors were imitating their own influential teachers. Reinventing their own interpretations of creative writing classroom lore in a field that as a whole rejects notions of itself as an academic discipline, they had little choice but to construct their own pedagogies in a vacuum. At best, such conditions resulted in a patchwork pedagogy with little basis in theory or practical research. At worst it encouraged a seat of the pants approach to teaching that eschews syllabi, class plans, and systematic assessment. Indeed, such a state of affairs perpetually situates

---

[1]Portions of this essay appeared in Kelly Ritter and Stephanie Vanderslice. "Teaching Lore: Creative Writers and the University." *Profession 2005*: 102–12.

the creative writing classroom in some parallel, anti-professional universe, often separated from the rest of a student's college coursework. In other courses, it is usually possible to see the path of instruction, the shape of the discipline, and the skeleton of pedagogy. In other courses, one can visualize the overall aims of the course and how it relates to other areas within the university (even if only as part of a general education paradigm common to all underclassmen). Creative writing courses, as they exist today, continue to be more difficult to puzzle out.

Of course, quality of instruction in all disciplines varies, and teachers spend their lives working on what might someday be the "perfect" way to run a classroom, to reach students, to change intellectual lives. But creative writing was and is *different*, special, outside the norm of these teaching challenges and professional questions. Rather than believe that difference, strangeness, other-worldliness is "just the way things are," or go to the other extreme and celebrate it (as many do), we would rather ask a simple, yet difficult, question: Why is this so?

Morris Freedman, in a 1960 issue of *College Composition and Communication*, notes:

> [The] highly commercialized teaching of creative writing, the teaching of it in myriads of separated little vacuums, is in its own shabby way big business and really has only remotely to do with the work of English departments. Yet it does seem to govern academic practice. Many colleges and universities seal themselves off from this plague outside their walls and have nothing whatsoever to do with creative writing. . . I myself have come to believe that creative writing courses have a valuable and inevitable place in the context of the *normal work* of a department of English. Certainly writing can no more be taught than painting or any skill in any art, but it *can be taught* as much. (Freedman 22, emphasis added).

These observations evidence the long history of creative writing as a marginalized discipline within English Studies. Morris asserts that creative writing (including its for-profit conferences and institutes) constitutes "big business," and that institutions, seeing their overall work as more "intellectual" or academic in nature, deliberately separate themselves from this teaching business. These assertions still ring true today, even as the shape of the modern English department has changed dramatically to include other similarly "fringe" concentrations such as film studies, cultural studies, and gay and lesbian studies. In today's university, which welcomes a diversity of fields in order to accommodate a shifting popular notion of higher education's purpose, creative writing remains a separatist site of teaching and learning, whose practice and traditions are rooted in a powerful lore that sustains such separation, with negative results for both faculty and students.

Such lore starts from the top and trickles down into creative writing program design, and then to individual students and faculty in those programs, becoming an unquestioned pattern of practice for generations of writers in

America. Creative writing has had a problematic history in the academy; this sometimes stems from prejudice from those in other disciplines who do not consider creative writing serious and scholarly. However, even as creative writing as a field recognizes that its disciplinary and accompanying faculty status is at issue in most universities, there exists a temptation to further marginalize creative writers as they seek to become respected university *teaching* faculty. This temptation often comes from within the faculty and programs themselves. Such self-marginalization in creative writing is largely related to the absence of teacher training and pedagogical reform in the face of the lore that perpetuates the traditions and customs of the field. Indeed, the lore of teaching creative writing—that which positions the teaching of creative writing as a favorite hand-me-down in the clothes closet of academia—is systemic, pervasive, and rooted in creative writing's isolated academic status, at once frustrating and comforting to the writers and organizations who perpetuate it. However, as much as that isolationist stance adversely affects public perception of writers as working professionals and community members, it affects the *teaching* of creative writing more—not just for students, but also for faculty who wish to develop as teachers.

With a few recent and noteworthy exceptions (Katherine Haake's *What Our Speech Disrupts: Feminism and Creative Writing Studies*, Anna Leahy's collection *Power and Identity in the Creative Writing Classroom: The Authority Project*, and Tim Mayers's *ReWriting Craft: Composition, Creative Writing and the Future of English Studies*), the prominent scholarship in creative writing has focused on either practical lesson plans for "how to" teach creative writing or has simply catalogued the history of creative writing as a discipline. Both approaches fail to question that pedagogy and history in relation to graduate program design and undergraduate curriculum development, as well as to the professional development of creative writers. The scholarship also fails to examine the importance of lore, which Stephen North defined as "the accumulated body of traditions, practices, and beliefs . . . that influence how writing is done, learned and taught" (22) and Ted Lardner described in the context of creative writing as "recipe-swapping" (i.e., try it this way, it works) (74). Many recent essays on creative writing instead emphasize the personal aspect of becoming a teacher and the obstacles one must overcome to (1) be taken seriously in an English department; (2) teach the mass of students who flock to creative writing courses, often without "talent"; and (3) continue as a "productive" writer while undertaking the "burden" of teaching writing. A pedagogy based solely on these types of essays might lead the uninitiated to ask, as Paul Dawson does, 'Is the pedagogical process merely guided by the idiosyncrasies of each teacher, the practicing writer able to pass on knowledge by virtue of his or her innate talent and secret knowledge of the craft?" ("Towards a New Poetic" 1).

The notion that teaching is a burden distinct from the act of writing, or that it is a "job" that writers do on the side, is reflected in many creative writing professors' narratives about the field. For example, Kenneth Hopkins, in his personal essay, "Amateur Professor," relates that upon taking a creative writing teaching job at SIU-Carbondale, his productivity ironically *increased* because he "was under no writing pressures—these were reserved for my students. The result is that in ten years I produced as many poems as I had produced in the previous thirty. . . in one year. . . I wrote 150 poems, not counting three which I wrote when I was drunk" (411). Hopkins comparatively relates that his "class met twice a week and the rest of the time was my own, apart from the necessity to read the work my students produced, not an exciting task."

What is striking about this narrative is the explicit separation of the identity of "writer" from that of "teacher." Hopkins deliberately divorces his teaching duties from his writing duties as part of a work week; the former being unexciting, burdensome work that pays the bills and funds his poetry. He uses his teaching experience as a backdrop for illustrating how *he* has changed as a writer. Narratives such as this define teaching as a task instead of an intellectually satisfying vocation. They don't discuss the relationship between teaching and writing as anything other than circumstance-driven.

Wendy Bishop, on the other hand, made a strong case for the intellectual satisfactions of a career that combines teaching and writing as a foundation of her scholarship in creative writing pedagogy; hers is the rare entry that connects teaching and writing as complementary and professionally rewarding activities. "I teach writing," Bishop proclaimed in an essay exploring the "identity" of the writer-teacher/teacher-writer, "precisely because I love these two intimately connected activities. Some days I am a writer who teaches (WT) and on the others, I am a teacher who writes (TW) but inevitably, I am one or the other" (14). She acknowledged, however, that in the academy this identity is a complicated one at best, one which she likened to a "sporting battle . . . the writers and critics [are] like two home town high school teams, challenging each other until they unite against a common enemy—teaching" (18).

Many essays that do explore the teaching of creative writing sidestep scholarship. Most of these are "stories"—literally *lore*—rather than contextualized discussions of teaching as a profession or analyses that relate theories of writing to theories of teaching. As Peter Vandenberg asserts, creative writing is "an institutional space that, owing to the benign neglect of literary studies and its own historical movement away from a scholarly discourse, has been ripe territory for annexation" (7). Indeed, this "annexation" is the exact situation that we fear creative writing professionals have initiated, and then locked themselves into and continually reinforce by embracing and exemplifying lore in their classrooms and their published tales of teaching writing.

This annexed space marginalizes all creative writing teachers, even those who embrace the intellectual community of teacher scholars. In further discussing lore in the context of pedagogy, North describes its "pragmatic logic and experience-based structure," and details its three most important functional properties (24). The first is that "literally anything can become a part of lore . . . once somebody says [something] has worked or is working or might work, it is part of lore" (24). The second, perhaps more troubling, property is that "while anything can become a part of lore, nothing can be dropped from it, either. There is simply no mechanism for it" (24). Thus, a field whose teaching practices and theories are relatively unexamined runs the risk of being dominated by an ever more unwieldy body of knowledge and practices, some of which have likely outgrown their usefulness or been misapplied. For example, the template of the graduate creative writing workshop, which Patrick Bizzaro refers to as a "model of instruction over a hundred years old but basically unrevised" (296), is often applied to the vastly different populations of the undergraduate creative writing course, with mixed results at best.

North's third property is that lore grows through accretion: "Once a nomination is made the contributor gives up control over it" (25) leaving it subject to "tinkering" by other practitioners who mold it, for better or worse, to suit their needs. While such modification can improve the original technique, it can just as easily lead to misapplication [consider the various transmutations of Peter Elbow's landmark conception of "freewriting" (25)]. Nonetheless, North believes that "lores in general . . . are clearly rich and powerful bodies of knowledge" (27), bodies of knowledge with untapped potential that can be unleashed only when those who perpetuate and defend it can argue "for the value of what they know and how they come to know it" (55). Such arguments require that practitioners first reflect upon, examine, and challenge their own institutionally inherited practices in the interests of rendering them more robust.

Even the landmark texts that survey the history of the field, such as D. G. Myers's *The Elephants Teach* and Joseph Moxley's *Creative Writing in America*, fall short of questioning traditional notions of the creative writing classroom as a space that privileges artistic production over intellectual development. While offering an exceptionally thorough examination of the history of creative writers and creative writing in academia and providing a historiographic look at the age-old, lore-laden question "Can creative writing be taught?" Myers's book charts creative writing's history only into the 1990s. Further, it fails to examine teaching in any depth beyond a continual nod to the "traditional horror of mixing pedagogy and creativity" (Wilson quoted in Myers 151) that only serves to further embed this concept as a persistent feature of the profession since its inception as a motto of the Iowa Writer's Workshop (i.e., writing cannot be taught but talent can be nurtured) (Dawson 3, Grimes 3). By failing to complicate and interrogate those traditions, studies such as Myers's perpetuate the model of the creative writing teacher as a mentor or "idol" whom younger writers should copy. Although one of many methods, it is the standard default position in creative writing pedagogy.

Other more recent collections, such as Wendy Bishop and Hans Ostrum's *Colors of a Different Horse,* come closer to establishing a critical dialogue about creative writing instruction in the university, but they focus on other issues, such as the value of creative writing's collaboration with other disciplines (i.e., composition) and alternative physical sites of writing instruction (such as the writing center), as well as concerns regarding the ethos of the teacher and the construction of that published writer outside the classroom. Bishop does pose a key question regarding the identity of writer-teachers and their creative writing classrooms in *Colors*, namely, ". . . to what extent does the craving itself [for artistic recognition] pollute teachers' perceptions of themselves and their classrooms?" (xiv).

Our book, however, takes on a more central mission. It asks teachers to reconsider commonly held assumptions about how student creative writers "learn" to write: whether they do so by imitation, modeling, the study of literature, the practicing of specific isolated strategies, or the almost magical development of innate talent. Based on this reconsideration, the various contributors to this book seek to know the best ways to teach creative writing and to nurture creative writers within a university setting—that is, to move beyond personal anecdote and myth.

The myths about writers in the academy have been touched upon in the past decade, notably in Ben Siegel's 1989 anthology *The American Writer and the University*. But this collection and others, such as Frank Conroy's *The Eleventh Draft*, mainly demonstrate how attitudes toward creative writing as an academic field permeate specific works of fiction and memoir about creative writing on campus, one popular and widely accessible site in which "lore" thrives. Collections such as these present pedagogical myths in the academy, which can be translated and interrogated as accepted lore.

As Siegel notes in his introduction, many academics argue that the creative artist is "simply an anomalous figure on campus. . . he or she is generally appointed to add a cultural veneer to the literature department and perhaps to attract students" (9). Here, Siegel sets up the familiar dichotomy between the "real" professor of literature and the "fake" professor of creative writing who masquerades as an academic. Whereas Siegel raises the issue of the writer as campus anomaly, we should question the need for a writer-teacher to be given this label at all. In a later chapter, David Madden points out that he is "distressed to hear many teachers of writing cater to the romantic preconceptions of the public and of students when they deny that writing (a mysterious process) can be taught, then go on to claim to achieve far more impossible goals—such as changing a student's life" (186). In other words, Madden laments the idea that creative writing is so esoteric and elusive as a discipline that its teaching must immediately transcend the practical and rise to the metaphysical or philosophical, in order to be validated as a vocation. The everpresent myth of the "unteachability" of creative writing is an important one, as it alone can separate the field from others in academia; in other words, if the subject can't be taught, why (and to what ends) are we teaching it.

Creative writing thus is continually re-inscribed as a romantic process that exists outside the boundaries of the classroom, although critics such as Tim Mayers and Gregory Light advocate for a craft-based pedagogy that pursues "newer, more effective ways to *teach* creative writing to students who might wish to learn it" (Mayers 84), Indeed, Light has gone so far as to design a broad-based research study on the development of hundreds of creative writers in writing programs across the United Kingdom, including the august University of East Anglia (Britain's equivalent to the Iowa Writers' Workshop), which revealed a statistically vigorous series of developmental stages through which writers progressed as they "learned" their craft. Such research dismantles the widely accepted myths that perpetuate stereotypes of creative writing as anything less than a "real" field in the university, allowing us to build on the foundation of creative writing as an uncontested teaching subject.

Finally, as Theodore Weiss notes in his contribution to Siegel's collection, writers are rarely seen as true faculty, with other non-writing faculty wondering ". . . how could they [creative writers] be expected to honor the regularities essential to the classroom or to deal objectively with students?" (152). This socially charged piece of lore—that creative writing faculty are less than trustworthy, perhaps due to their patrician upbringing, which separates them from the mass of students in their charge—might best be interrogated by writing professionals who themselves come from working-class backgrounds and were trained as both scholars and writers. We must interrogate this myth of the writer-at-a-distance, for example, by examining how artifacts of our popular culture (novels, films) shape the myth of the reclusive and eccentric writer, subsequently glorifying these archetypes in the classroom.

We can also galvanize the field by reassessing specific patterns and practices in our creative writing programs, including

- The cyclical use of language and power that academic lore perpetuates inside and outside the creative writing classroom, particularly in those programs that are highly ranked and thus are financial and intellectual centers of prosperity for their home universities;

- The avoidance of critical and cultural theory in creative writing classrooms;

- The notion that creative writing cannot be evaluated objectively;

- The writing workshop, the staple of creative writing programs and classrooms since the adoption of the Iowa model;

- The role of popular culture, including the role of canonical titles such as John Gardner's *The Art of Fiction*, with their iron-clad prescriptions for a successful writing life.

Behind our collective pedagogies as teachers of creative writing lies a collective history of learning fueled by lore; to ignore this history and its deceptively simple construction does a great disservice to the field. Existing scholarship ignores the lore of creative writing pedagogy, considering it to be only small, uncomplicated utterances, when in fact it is a powerful, complicated discourse, one whose power we will harness only by giving it our full critical response.

How *Can It Really Be Taught* Came to Be and What We Hope It Will Do

After our first meeting, at the MFA Special Interest Group at the four C's in spring 2001 with the Colorado Rockies as our backdrop, we began an epistolary collaboration in which we exchanged ideas and research—our own and that of others—and shared our visions for creative writing in higher education, where it had been and where we felt it needed to go. We knew that examining creative writing "lore" as Stephen North defined it could be potentially transformative for the discipline and first considered tackling the subject ourselves in a co-authored book. However, as we delved into the subject more deeply we recognized that its latent range and power all but demanded consideration by a plurality of voices. Consequently, while we had our own list of "usual suspects" of creative writing lore, in our initial call for essays we asked authors to propose their own interpretations of the myths of the field in which they wrote, studied, and taught. In much the same way that a teacher expects a lively debate when she turns class discussion over to a particularly dynamic group, we hoped that those who answered our call would discover instances of lore that we had not even considered and not only illuminate but interrogate them.

Indeed, our contributors have shed light on some uncharted territory—for example, the myth of the writer depicted in film or the complicated assumptions implied by popular creative writing texts—as well as some more familiar sites, such as the persistent myth of the creative writing course as an easy "A." In every case, these authors have struggled mightily with the contexts of these sites of lore and their implications for creative writing pedagogy. Moreover, in the end they reveal ways in which they have mitigated the influence of such lore in their own classrooms and in their own teaching and writing lives, so that interested readers may do the same.

A defining characteristic of lore is that it has become so deeply embedded in the culture that practices it that it is part of the basic assumptions of that culture, in this case, all but invisible to those who teach and write in the world it scaffolds. While certainly a modicum of comfort resides in the proclamation, "it has always been thus and thus it always shall be, time immemorial," so does a degree of dangerous complacency. You hold in your hands a collection of essays designed to make you think about those assumptions that constitute the way you teach creative writing and the way you were taught, about what it means to be a writer as well as a teacher and a student of writing both inside and outside the academy today. As you consider the creative writing students awaiting your presence tomorrow morning or even those you will teach next semester, this collection is intended to make you wonder, "Where does this theory come from?" "Is this practice effective?" "How so?" "What will happen if I try it differently next time?"

Perhaps you will take issue with an assertion in one of these essays or perhaps, even better, this collection will inspire you to write about a creative writing myth that has not been illuminated in these pages, extending the conversation we have begun. Rich conversations such as these will affirm that there is ample room for the discipline of creative writing at the English studies table, so long as that discipline is not a static one where protocols have been reinscribed for decades. Rather it must be a discipline of productive, critical conversation in which every teacher is encouraged to join, to take responsibility for what happens in his or her classroom through vigorous reflection on theory and practice; a discipline in which myths are not habitually propagated and the cult of personality that often blooms among them is checked at the door.

Finally, the purpose of this book is *not* just to say; it is to question, to provoke, to account for and, ultimately, to endanger the propagation of unexamined lore in our creative writing classrooms.

Bibliography

Bishop, Wendy. 1999. "Places to Stand: The Reflective Writer-Teacher-Writer in Composition." *College Composition and Communication* 51.1(Sept.): 9–31.

———. 1994. *Colors of a Different Horse: Rethinking Creative Writing Theory and Pedagogy.* Urbana, IL: NCTE.

Bizarro, Patrick. 2004. "Research and Reflection in English Studies: The Special Case of Creative Writing." *College English* 66.3 (Jan.): 294–309.

Dawson, Paul. 2005. "Towards a New Poetics in Creative Writing Pedagogy." *TEXT* 7.1 (April): 1–15.

Freedman, Morris. 1960. "The Proper Place of Creative Writing Courses." *College Composition and Communication* 11.1 (Feb.): 22–26.

Grimes, Tom. 1999. "Workshop and the Writing Life." *The Workshop: Seven Decades of the Iowa Writers' Workshop.* New York: Hyperion, pp. 1–15.

Guillory, John. 2002. "The Very Idea of Pedagogy." *Profession 2002* (Winter): 164–71.

Haake, Katherine. 2000. *What Our Speech Disrupts: Feminism and Creative Writing Studies.* Carbondale: NCTE.

Hopkins, Kenneth. 1990. "Amateur Professor." *Papers on Language and Literature* 26.3 (Summer): 407–24.

Lardner, Ted. 1999. "Locating the Boundaries of Composition and Creative Writing." *College Composition and Communication* 51.1(Sept.): 9–31.

Leahy, Anna. 2005. *Power and Identity in the Creative Writing Classroom: The Authority Project.* Clevedon: Multilingual Matters.

Light, Gregory. 2002. "Conceiving Creative Writing in Higher Education." http://19. . ./action.lasso?database=nawearchive&layout=internet7response=archive2.html& recID=3 2933&. Accessed March 4, 2002.

———. 2002. "From the Personal to the Public: Conceptions of Creative Writing in Higher Education." *Higher Education* 43.2 (March): 257–77.

Mayers, Tim. 1999. "ReWriting Craft." *College Composition and Communication* 51.1 (Sept.): 9–31.

————. 2005. *(RE) Writing Craft: Composition, Creative Writing, and the Future of English Studies.* Pittsburgh: University of Pittsburgh Press.

Myers, D. G. 1996. *The Elephants Teach: Creative Writing Since 1880.* Englewood Cliffs, NJ: Prentice Hall.

North, Stephen M. 1987. *The Making of Knowledge in Composition: Portrait of an Emerging Field.* Portsmouth, NH: Boynton/Cook, Heinemann.

Siegel, Ben. 1989. *The American Writer and the University.* Newark: University of Delaware Press.

Vandenberg, Peter. 2004. "Integrated Writing Programmes in American Universities: Whither Creative Writing?" *New Writing: An International Journal for the Practice and   Theory of Creative Writing* 1.1:1–13.

1

Figuring the Future

Lore and/in Creative Writing

By Tim Mayers

Creative writers in college and university English departments have most often existed professionally in terms quite different from those of their departmental colleagues. Although this has begun to change, albeit quite slowly, creative writers still frequently exist in a type of privileged marginality, mostly left alone to do what they do best—write—and teach aspiring young writers the tools of the trade. Their classes operate on the workshop model; at each class meeting, they discuss one or more pieces of student writing in an attempt to help the student writers make these pieces better—that is, more like "professional," published pieces. The creative writers may have only tenuous ties to their colleagues in other parts of the English department. They may be wary of colleagues who specialize in literature, believing that these colleagues' fascination with theory and analysis sucks the spirit out of the works they read (at best), or demonstrates an open hostility to these works (at worst). The creative writers may joke among themselves that the critic-types are all just frustrated writers anyway, those who just didn't have what it takes to succeed, and who now nag those writers who did make it.

The creative writers may be equally wary of their colleagues in composition. They shudder at the thought of classrooms full of grammatically—and aesthetically—impaired students who, the institution proclaims, need to be taught how to write. They wonder how compositionists can go on about pedagogy when it seems so obvious that these students just aren't writers—never have been, never will be—and that no amount of teaching, no matter how well-intentioned, is ever going to change that. The compositionists, for their part, may not pay much attention to the creative writers unless they cause trouble at department meetings. The literature specialists and the compositionists may debate the relative status of their fields, or whether literary texts have a proper place in the composition classroom. In these debates, creative writers are largely kept out of the mix. And too often, everyone seems happy to have it that way.

Creative writers, in other words, live in a professional world characterized by "lore," something all the contributors to this volume believe to be well worth examining. The concept of "lore" has carried key-word status in the discourse of composition studies since Stephen M. North first described it in 1987. Lore is associated with "Practitioners," whose primary professional identities are as teachers, not necessarily scholars, of composition. Lore is "the accumulated body of traditions, practices, and beliefs in terms of which Practitioners understand how writing is done, learned, and taught" (North 22). North's description of lore marked a crucial moment in the development of composition studies, allowing a much fuller and clearer articulation of the field than had been previously possible, and—perhaps more importantly— opening up new avenues for development. Patricia Harkin has provocatively explored both the limits and the possibilities of lore as a form of inquiry in composition, noting that it is "nondisciplinary . . . actually defined by its inattention to disciplinary procedures" (125) but also potentially "postdisciplinary" (126–27) or capable, at least in some circumstances, of usefully addressing pedagogical problems for which the traditional limits of disciplinary inquiry would be too constraining. This volume, published nearly two decades after North's *The Making of Knowledge in Composition,* has the potential to mark a similar moment in the development of creative writing.

Yet to equate the lore of composition with the lore of creative writing would be a grave mistake. Institutional history has led the two fields to very different places. And although there exists now, I believe, the potential for an institutional alliance between composition and creative writing that would have far-reaching implications for the future of English studies in general, the current differences between them cannot be simply glossed over. Instead, they must be understood and articulated within their institutional contexts.

The "Conventional Wisdom" of Creative Writing

From the outside, creative writing may appear to be a field in which teaching is of paramount importance; thus, many observers might be initially surprised by the relative dearth of published material about creative writing pedagogy. There are several exceptions to this general rule, most notably Wendy Bishop's *Released Into Language: Options for Teaching Creative Writing* (1990), Mary Ann Cain's *Revisioning Writers' Talk: Gender and Culture in Acts of Composing* (1995), and Katharine Haake's *What Our Speech Disrupts: Feminism and Creative Writing Studies* (2000). Yet the rarity of such efforts becomes understandable if we consider the historical investment of creative writing in notions that render pedagogy largely unworthy of serious exploration. Patrick Bizzaro offers the following anecdote in a review essay: After presenting a paper on creative writing pedagogy at the Association of Writers and Writing

Programs' (AWP) annual convention, Bizzaro was approached by "a poet acquaintance" who "explained that she was of the opinion that real writers spend their time writing, and that AWP's Pedagogy Forum wasn't really taken seriously by writers anyway. . . . Creative writers, she insisted, 'don't give papers at conferences'" (286). Bizzaro's colleague's invocation of the term "real writers," and the context in which the term is used, point toward what might be called the "conventional wisdom" of creative writing—a cluster of rarely articulated assumptions about what writing is, whether or not it can be taught, and what kinds of people qualify as writers.[1] In the terms of this volume, creative writing's conventional wisdom would be virtually synonymous with creative writing's lore.

We might push this conventional wisdom—this lore—toward fuller articulation here by considering a few other sources. Perhaps it is best summed up by Ron McFarland, who writes (in the only *College English* article published during the 1990s devoted entirely to creative writing), "I once ascertained five essentials of a serious writer: desire, drive, talent, vision, and craft. . . . My point . . . is not altered whether the list is held at five, cut to three, or expanded to twenty: of the essentials, only craft can be taught" (34). Lurking beneath the surface of this statement is a whole cluster of assumptions about writers and writing—a cluster of assumptions too intricate to unpack here. W. Ross Winterowd, however, provides a cogent summary of the intellectual currents that might lead to a position such as McFarland's: "Invention [has] been split, with creative genius leading the poet into Sidney's golden world while method [leaves] the composition student in the brazen world of the quotidian. With invention transformed to creativity or the originary genius of the poet, rhetoric [is] left with a managerial as opposed to a creative or generative function" (75). Elsewhere, Winterowd calls this the Romantic legacy within English departments, characterized by —among other things—the notion that one either is or is not a writer, and that this cannot be changed by any amount of schooling. Or, as the poet Mary Oliver begins a recent book, "Everyone knows that poets are born and not made in school. . . . This book is about the things that *can* be learned. It is about matters of *craft*" (1, emphasis mine). Craft, though not explicitly defined by McFarland or Oliver, entails for both of them that (very small) part of creative writing that lies outside—or at least at the border of—the realm of genius. To put this a different way, craft is the faint gray area of overlap between genius and rhetoric. One cannot be taught to be a genius, but one can learn to imitate some of the techniques in which geniuses are expert. This, as I will argue later, is a reductive and devalued version of craft, one that needs to be seriously reconsidered.

As I have previously suggested, lore in composition constructs a professional identity for practitioners as teachers; while writing or composition is

---

[1]In *(Re)Writing Craft: Composition, Creative Writing, and the Future of English Studies*, I describe "the institutional-conventional wisdom of creative writing" in much more detail.

that which gets taught, the primary identity of the practitioner is as *teacher*. This is not the case with creative writing. In creative writing, *writer* is the primary identity; *teacher* is secondary. This part of creative writing's lore is actually spelled out specifically by the Association of Writers and Writing Programs, creative writing's major professional organization. In the "Values and Beliefs" section of its *Strategic Plan 2000 – 2010*, the AWP specifically defines itself as the province of "writers who teach," thereby elevating the former identity over the latter. More specifically: "AWP believes that those accomplished in making literature are the most effective teachers of writing and literature" (11). This statement would probably make most composition-ists cringe, not only because it is unsubstantiated, but also because it contra-dicts so much of the knowledge about pedagogy developed within composi-tion studies. AWP's argument seems specious, too, when considered in light of comparable situations. For example, while some great athletes eventually become great athletic coaches, many fail miserably at coaching. The same is true for artists and musicians. It would seem, then, that AWP's position on writers as teachers needs to be complicated or challenged if creative writing is to develop modes of pedagogical and theoretical inquiry as rich and diverse as those in composition studies.

Another aspect of creative writing's conventional wisdom or lore is the ten-dency to think of fiction and poetry in artistic rather than rhetorical terms. The type of writing most creative writers aspire toward is not sullied by involvement with political, economic, or social concerns. It exists, first and foremost, for its own sake, and aims at timelessness, or a transcendence of the concerns of the everyday. The primary aim or purpose of composing, within this schema, is to produce the work itself, and not to have that work *do* anything, such as persuade or inform an audience. The pursuit of publications and prizes (and even, at times, academic jobs) might seem at first glance to be an aim of this sort of writ-ing, but creative writing's conventional wisdom holds that these things are merely by-products of the quality of the writing—and the writer.

This conventional wisdom enmeshes creative writing in a number of contradictions. On one hand the field is democratic, viewing literature as not only a collection of historically great texts, but also as an ongoing activity to which newcomers might make significant contributions. On the other hand, creative writing is elitist, identifying in the end only a select few students who might be worthy of the label of "real writer." Many creative writing teachers, in fact, believe it is their duty to identify and nurture these rare and delicate creatures, while at the same time gently bringing other young hopefuls to the realization that they will never really amount to anything, at least as writers. Frequently, this judgment may be passed *before* a student even gets to enter a creative writing classroom. At colleges and universities where student demand for creative writing courses outpaces the English department's ability (or will-ingness) to staff sections with instructors, students must often submit a port-folio of writing samples in order to be approved to register for the course.

Student writers judged by the instructor to be inadequately talented or prepared are not allowed to take the course.

As I will demonstrate later, however, not all creative writers accept this
conventional wisdom, and challenges to the conventional wisdom—not
always meant to discredit it, but perhaps sometimes to complicate or enrich
it—may well open up a space for creative writing to be more fully integrated
with composition, and perhaps also with literary studies. Alternatively, an
alliance between composition and creative writing may lead the fields to
separate themselves from literary studies. Ultimately, such things will be
decided as the need arises. For the purposes of my argument now, though, a
further exploration is in order, an exploration of institutional and historical
factors that have both helped to create and to sustain the lore of creative writing as I have been describing it here.

Reading the Past, Writing the Future

Because creative writing (as an academic endeavor) has almost always been
housed in English departments, it must be understood in terms of its connections and disconnections to English studies. The histories and futures of English studies are inextricably bound up with each other. Studies of particular
histories of English studies are often motivated by a desire for a clearer understanding of the present, an understanding of how things got to be the way they
are. Such an understanding, in turn, is sought because of a desire for change,
a desire to shape the direction of the future. Unfortunately, much of the existing scholarship on the histories and futures of English studies suffers from a
glaring flaw: the assumption that English studies can be roughly divided into
two camps or fields—literature and composition. Under this guiding assumption, histories often play out as conflicts between the two camps, and futures
are usually imagined as negotiated settlements between them. This assumption is flawed, I believe, because it ignores or passes over the role of a third
field within English studies—creative writing—which has played an important
part in the histories of many individual English departments during the twentieth and twenty-first centuries. Because it is not quite the same thing as literature or composition, and because it is simultaneously similar to and different
from each, creative writing can offer unique perspectives on where English
departments have come from, and where they might go.

During the past fifteen years or so, scholarship on the histories and futures
of English studies, written mainly by those affiliated with composition and
rhetoric, has become perhaps the most exciting subspecialty within the discipline.
Scholars, both emerging and established, have turned their attention toward
the many ways in which college English has become what it is, and offered
many proposals for how it might be redesigned as it moves into the twenty-
first century. At this point, I would like to look briefly at three representative
examples of such scholarship from the late 1990s to point out the vital

importance of work in the area, and to highlight the above-mentioned flawed tendency in much of this discourse, a tendency I believe needs to be corrected if scholarship on the histories and futures of English studies is to remain as intellectually exciting and politically valuable as it has been.

James A. Berlin's *Rhetorics, Poetics, and Cultures: Refiguring College English Studies* (1996), Sharon Crowley's *Composition in the University: Historical and Polemical Essays* (1998), and W. Ross Winterowd's *The English Department: A Personal and Institutional History* (1998) are books that share important similarities. All are by established and widely respected scholars who harbor a genuine interest in the health of English studies. All examine historical and ideological reasons why English studies has developed into its present incarnations. But history, in these volumes, is not pursued merely for its own sake, as Berlin, Crowley, and Winterowd all offer specific proposals for redesigning English studies to correct the mistakes of the past and ensure a more viable field for the future. Unfortunately, though, all of these books also remain largely rooted in a reductivist tendency that has marred virtually all of the scholarship on the histories and futures of English studies up to this point. Specifically, these three scholars persist in dividing English studies (far too neatly) in half, between literature and composition, leaving creative writing (and, in fact, other areas of study as well) outside the realm of analysis. To their credit, all of these scholars make tentative gestures toward moving away from this tendency,[2] but nonetheless offer creative writing far less attention than it deserves, given the sheer number of creative writing undergraduate and graduate courses and degrees offered by English departments across America (see, for example, Myers 166).

The Triple Division of English Studies

As I have already mentioned, most of the scholars who attempt to refigure English studies view English as a field divided in two, between literature and composition. This tendency is even more striking in books published earlier than those I have mentioned (see, for example, James Berlin's earlier histories of writing instruction in America and Susan Miller's *Textual Carnivals: The Politics of Composition* [1991]). But I believe it is far more accurate to regard English as a field divided into at least three parts—literature, composition, and creative writing.[3] D. G. Myers, in his history of creative writing

[2]Berlin, for example, points out how the critical work of a few creative writers might fit into his vision of a refigured English department (162-68). Winterowd notes how the Romantic legacy within English departments, inherited from figures such as Coleridge and Emerson, effectively splits composition apart from creative writing and relegates composition to a lower status (167). And Crowley also mentions creative writing occasionally in her analyses of the "status relationship" between literature and composition.

[3]Even this triple division may not adequately account for all of the activities housed within English departments, which may also include linguistics, ESL, English education, and theater. Still, the notion of a three-way split offers far richer possibilities for analysis than the binary literature/composition split.

in America, offers an excellent and cogent critique of this tendency among scholars to divide English studies in half, whether that division is literature vs. composition, reading vs. writing, or interpretation vs. production. Myers finds this two-part division inadequate to describe what has gone on historically within English studies. "What I am suggesting is that historically there has been a three-way split in English departments: the terrain has been carved up into sectors representing scholarship, social practices, and what I am going to refer to as constructivism" (Myers 9). Myers goes on to note that

> I am going to base my own historical analysis on the premise that scholarly research in English, the teaching of practical composition, and constructivist handling of literature are three distinct 'faculties' of study, thought, and activity in English, differentiated by aim and method, by the uses to which they put their materials, at times even unrelated to each other. . . . English itself is not a consistent order; its existence is bureaucratic (or "economic," if you prefer), not logical . . . it is less a name than the designation of a plurality of interests. For historical reasons, English has become home to several logically indistinguishable and perhaps even mutually incompatible modes of activity. (10)

For this line of argument alone, *The Elephants Teach* is a crucially important contribution to the history of English studies. It opens up the possibility that English studies might be analyzed not in terms of an ongoing battle between two rival camps, but rather as a constantly shifting coexistence of three ideologies, each of which is bureaucratically, economically, and institutionally inscribed within particular departments, and each of which occasionally overlaps with one or more of the others. But because his interests are primarily historical, Myers focuses almost exclusively on how things got to be the way they are and leaves unanswered the question of where things might be headed. Also, Myers's disappointment with what creative writing has become—an "elephant machine," an institutional substructure devoted almost entirely to reproducing itself—leaves him either unwilling or unable to entertain the possibility that creative writing might be more fully integrated with composition or literary study. So while I applaud Myers's critique of the binary split in most histories of English studies, I wish to differ with him about what creative writing should become. In short, I would like to see creative writing enter into a productive dialogue with other fields of English studies, especially composition. This will require significant changes in the way most creative writers view themselves and their students as writers, and in their willingness to question and challenge their place within the hierarchies of English studies. Creative writers in academia must be willing to reassess the conventional wisdom—the lore—that has long provided a foundation for both theory and practice in creative writing classrooms.

Theory and Practice in Creative Writing
and Composition

It may be helpful to sum up, in broader historical and institutional terms, what I have argued thus far. From one perspective, the institutional separation of creative writing and composition seems extremely odd. Both endeavors, after all, involve teaching students to produce texts. For ideological and historical reasons, though, creative writing and composition have developed into separate (and very different) institutional enterprises. The gulf between these two strands of English studies has widened in the past twenty to thirty years, with composition moving steadily toward (if in fact it has not already achieved) status as a full-fledged academic discipline (or subdiscipline), and creative writing becoming an almost anti-academic endeavor, existing within the academy essentially by default, because there seems to be no other hospitable place for it. In composition, pedagogy has become a thriving area of study in its own right, and pedagogical theories—even deeply incompatible ones—come into dialectic engagement at regional and national conferences, in the pages of composition journals, and in electronic media such as listserv discussions. In creative writing, pedagogy is (on the surface at least) far less problematic and far less open to question. The workshop model, developed at the University of Iowa and a few other schools during the 1940s and 1950s, remains the dominant pedagogical model in creative writing classrooms across the country. Patrick Bizzaro notes that creative writers have long "held to a model of instruction . . . without giving it proper scrutiny." Yet Bizzaro also imagines that there are many creative writers, like him, interested in pedagogy and eager to discuss and debate it (287).

It would be worthwhile, though, to re-articulate why there might be such a marked difference regarding pedagogy in the two fields, to consider which interests are served by the continual reproduction of the workshop model and the devaluation of pedagogy in creative writing. The reasons, I think, are several. First, creative writers' investment in the notion that writers are born and not made makes the whole issue of pedagogy suspect from the outset. For if writers cannot be made, no amount of teaching will "work," at least for those who are not already writers. The question then becomes: What kinds of things should or can be taught to those who are not writers, and how do we identify and nurture those who do seem to be writers? Second, many creative writers, if they consider themselves the kind of "real writers" previously mentioned, do not consider teaching part of their primary identity. Teaching is something they do to pay the bills; it is a profession that at least allows *some* time for writing, and perhaps even a strong incentive to publish. When they do teach, many creative writers rely on the workshop model simply because it is the only model they have ever known; all of their formal training as writers is likely to have occurred in workshops. But if they could make a living by writing alone, many creative writers might choose to do so. Third, most creative writers in academia are expected (or believe they are expected) to publish stories, poems, and novels—not to write books on pedagogy, not to present papers at conferences. In short, the lack of explicit attention to pedagogy allows many creative writers to consider themselves writers who teach, rather than teachers who write, and to embrace that version of their identity through the auspices of the AWP.

Creative Writing, Composition, and the Question of Craft

"Craft," perhaps the most pervasive and ill-defined term within the lore of creative writing, might well be a key word around which creative writers and compositionists can stake out a territory of shared concern. This will be no easy task, as it will require a casting aside of deeply rooted prejudices and animosities. It will, however, be a worthwhile task, as I believe an alliance between creative writing and composition might provide energy and institutional power for both fields. W. Ross Winterowd envisions such an alliance toward the end of his book *The English Department*, imagining a writing program that would include instruction in, and opportunities for informal discussion about, all kinds of writing. Winterowd explains the importance of this shift as follows:

> In the [redesigned] writing center and program, words such as *imagination* and *creativity* would be . . . replaced by *craft*. The basis of all art is craft, and when the focus is on craft, when craft is honored, such lowly concerns as sentence structure and document design (typography, effective subheads, organizational strategies) gain value that they do not have when imagination is the god-term, yet it is often craft that makes the difference between an effective and an ineffective text, a text that does what an author intends and a text which does not accomplish its purpose. (229, italics in original)

Perhaps there is a problem here, though. Winterowd uses the term "craft" as though its meaning is self-evident. Yet craft is a term that has been completely compatible with the conventional wisdom and lore of creative writing, as entangled as that wisdom is in other concepts such as creativity, genius, and imagination. Romantic ideals devalue craft, I would argue, in much the same way they devalue rhetoric and "nonimaginative" composition—trends Winterowd rightfully denounces. I entirely agree with him that writing programs might be fruitfully reorganized around the concept of craft, but this concept needs to be redefined in order to become more capacious.

In this regard, Winterowd—or anyone engaged in a project such as the one he describes—might find valuable allies in a group of creative writers I call "craft critics," writers who question and challenge the prevailing, reductive notion of craft and attempt to make it a broader and more intellectually valuable area of concern.[4] Many of these craft critics find value in the later works of Martin Heidegger, who believed poetry to be closer than philosophy to the realm of genuine thinking. Heidegger sought to enlarge the notion of craft beyond its incarnation as "the mere manipulation of tools" and toward the extraordinarily complex relationship between the craftsperson and his or her medium—wood for cabinet-makers, canvas and paint for painters, language for writers, etc. (23). The ranks of craft critics include such writers as Sherod Santos, who questions the long-held belief that aspiring creative writers should be urged to "write about what they know" and envisions a pedagogy that might exploit the possibility that the composing process teaches us what we *don't* know, moving us toward hitherto undiscovered, and necessarily partial, truths. Heather McHugh, in *Broken English: Poetry and Partiality*, rejects the New Critical/Romantic/humanist notions of the intrinsic unity of both the poet and the poem. She prefers instead a (poststructuralist) concept of disunity and fragmentation, viewing composing as the act(s) of fragmented and multiple selves within the fragmented and multiple medium of language. Bob Perelman explores the possibility that mixed genres such as the poem/essay or prose poem might usefully intervene in both theoretical debates and in academic politics. And James Scully rejects the tendency of creative writing to value quietism and contemplation, exploring instead the possibility that poetry (and other so-called "creative" genres) can aid in the struggle for worldwide political transformation.

Probably the most provocative statement by any craft critic, at least for the purposes of this chapter, is the following one by Michael Heller, who comments on the task of the poet in the contemporary world:

> The poet needs . . . to cultivate, at minimum, a hypersensitivity to the "mythologies" of poetic craft, including those narcotics we call beauty, harmony, symmetry. In this sense, the poet cannot afford to be merely a literary figure. [The poet's] field of activity is the entire language production of the available culture. [The poet] must be acquainted with the discursive currents which operate in that culture, which valorize certain modes and denigrate others, which bring to prominence certain kinds of thinking or activities and significantly forget or neglect others. [The poet] must see these practices for what they are, not overarching truths (even though they may hold "truths") but forms of rhetoric or ideology. Indeed, a more complete understanding of rhetoric seems now to be essential to poesis. (15)

If poets (and other creative writers) in academia were to heed Heller's advice, they might well find themselves within the same orbit as their colleagues in composition and rhetoric. In arguing that writers can no longer afford to be "literary figures," I think Heller is lobbying for a shaking-off of

---

[4]I define craft criticism in much more detail, and provide numerous examples and discussions of it, in *(Re)Writing Craft*.

the Romantic and New Critical world-views in which so many creative writers have invested themselves. Not all creative writers, I suspect, will be willing to do this, but those who are could join their compositionist colleagues in attempting to make writing instruction, and theories of writing instruction, more valuable, valued, and intellectually respectable than they currently are in so many literature-dominated English departments.

Writing into the Future: Three Pleas for Action

During the past few years, the proliferation of books and articles addressing the histories and futures of English studies has served as ample evidence that many professionals who teach English have taken upon themselves the responsibility of ascertaining, as clearly as possible, how their field has developed into what it is, and of actively debating what it should become. This scholarship has been essential, I would argue, in helping both emerging and established professionals within the field understand (and at times transform) their teaching practices and theoretical predispositions. At the same time, scholars engaged in these examinations have too often posited a version of English studies that is neatly divided in half, between literature and composition. Historians of the discipline have tended either to ignore creative writing entirely or to give it only a passing mention. This, I think, must change. An interest in writing fiction or poetry, after all, is what draws many students into English studies in the first place. A desire to learn to write is certainly what led me into the field as an undergraduate. If, as many scholars have argued, we owe it to our present and future students to craft a more coherent and less fragmented version of English studies, then certainly the theory and practice of creative writing are not just interesting, but rather *essential*, areas of concern. My first plea, then, is to historians of English studies: While continuing your excellent investigations of composition instruction and literary studies, please turn your attention toward creative writing as well, particularly insofar as it has interacted (or in many cases, failed to interact) with other areas of the discipline.

My second plea is to those creative writers within academia who have effectively separated themselves from the discipline of English studies while remaining, nominally, under the umbrella of the English department and thereby enjoy the privileges available in such a position: Please come out of isolation and join a fascinating conversation. If, in fact, you believe your colleagues in literature and composition don't understand your concerns, why not clarify them and argue on their behalf? Instead of being content with the privileged and comfortable marginality in which you now exist, why not demand a place at the table? You will likely find that you have more in common with your colleagues than you think. And if you teach graduate students, consider the alarming shortage of academic jobs that allow for the teaching of creative writing only. Most of your students who find employment in the academy will have to teach something else in addition to, or instead of, creative writing.

Separating yourselves from colleagues elsewhere in the discipline, then, is a dramatic disservice to your students.

My third and final plea is to those engaged in redesigning college writing programs, both in theory and in practice. Please consider how creative writing might fit into a larger writing curriculum. James Berlin, Sharon Crowley, and W. Ross Winterowd have, each in their own ways, opened up such a possibility, arguing for curricula that would provide students with the opportunity to study and practice discourse production in varied and specific contexts. And a few writing programs, such as those at SUNY Albany and the University of Central Arkansas, have already begun to integrate creative writing instruction into curricula that include instruction in numerous other kinds of writing. All of these efforts are worth serious consideration. They promise to help create more adaptable and rhetorically aware student writers, writers whose knowledge of different genres and contexts allows them to succeed at multiple writing tasks. Also, these efforts at curricular transformation promise to help English studies remain as viable a field in the twenty-first century as it was in the twentieth. Creative writing, I believe, should be an important part of that field, but it will become and remain so only through the efforts of scholars and teachers determined to pay attention to what English studies has been in the past, is now at present, and might become as we move into the future.

Bibliography

Association of Writers & Writing Programs. *Strategic Plan 2000 – 2010.* Revised 2003.

Berlin, James A. 1996. *Rhetorics, Poetics, and Cultures: Refiguring College English Studies.* Urbana, IL: National Council of Teachers of English.

Bishop, Wendy. 1990. *Released Into Language: Options for Teaching Creative Writing.* Urbana, IL: National Council of Teachers of English.

Bizzaro, Patrick. 1998. "Should I Write This Essay or Finish a Poem? Teaching Writing Creatively." *College Composition and Communication* 49:2 (May): 285–97.

Cain, Mary Ann. 1995. *Revisioning Writers' Talk: Gender and Culture in Acts of Composing.* Albany: SUNY Press.

Crowley, Sharon. 1998. *Composition in the University: Historical and Polemical Essays.* Pittsburgh: University of Pittsburgh Press.

Haake, Katharine. 2000. *What Our Speech Disrupts: Feminism and Creative Writing Studies.* Urbana: National Council of Teachers of English.

Harkin, Patricia. 1991. "The Postdisciplinary Politics of Lore." In *Contending with Words: Composition and Rhetoric in a Postmodern Age.* Patricia Harkin and John Schilb, eds. New York: Modern Language Association, pp. 124–38.

Heidegger, Martin. 1968. *What Is Called Thinking?* Trans. J. Glenn Gray. New York: Harper & Row.

Heller, Michael. 1995. "The Uncertainty of the Poet." *American Poetry Review* 24:3 (May/June): 11–16.

Mayers, Tim. 2005. *(Re)Writing Craft: Composition, Creative Writing, and the Future of English Studies.* Pittsburgh: University of Pittsburgh Press.

McHugh, Heather. 1993. *Broken English: Poetry and Partiality.* Hanover, NH: University Press of New England.

Miller, Susan. 1991. *Textual Carnivals: The Politics of Composition.* Carbondale: Southern Illinois University Press.

Myers, D. G. 1996. *The Elephants Teach: Creative Writing Since 1880.* New York: Prentice Hall.

North, Stephen M. 1987. *The Making of Knowledge in Composition: Portrait of an Emerging Field.* Upper Montclair, NJ: Boynton.

Perelman, Bob. 1996. *The Marginalization of Poetry: Language Writing and Literary History.* Princeton, NJ: Princeton University Press.

Santos, Sherod. 1993. "Eating the Angel, Conceiving the Sun: Toward a Notion of Poetic Thought." *American Poetry Review* 22:6 (November/December): 9–13.

Scully, James. 1988. *Line Break: Poetry as Social Practice.* Seattle: Bay Press.

Winterowd, W. Ross. 1998. *The English Department: A Personal and Institutional History.* Carbondale: Southern Illinois University Press.

2

Against Reading

By Katharine Haake

Starting Out

When I was a new writer/teacher, emerging into the field more than twenty years ago, I took a good look at what Patrick Bizzaro describes as the "powerful and conservative throng of poets, novelists, and dramatists" (295) that dominated the field then as it does today and wondered how exactly I fit in. My feeling at the time—wandering the conference rooms of AWP, for example, or scanning publications for news of where I might place my work, or even inside my own classroom where whatever teaching models I might have relied on were quickly turning out to be insufficient—was not unlike the feelings I had as an adolescent reading *Moby Dick* and deciding, with a clarity of conviction I might never know again, that I was neither smart enough nor talented enough to be a writer. At the time, Linda Brodkey's work on the modernist scene of writing—a male author writing literature alone in his attic garret by the light of a thin gray candle—provided me a good deal of comfort. Maybe there wasn't anything especially lacking in me, but in the way that writing came into being and moved through the world. Maybe I was reading the signs wrong.

Today, I know that I was never as alone as I felt then. In "Who's the Teacher?: From Student to Mentor," Audrey Petty writes affectingly of her experience as a young teacher, an experience that persists today as far too common. Relying on longstanding habits of imitation, Petty had gone into her first creative writing classroom expecting to teach like her mentor before her, only to come up against the limitations of her body. She writes

> Within the first weeks of workshop, I painfully realized that I could not inhabit the same space my mentor/colleague did as a teacher. He taught as a storyteller. I couldn't. I couldn't tell long and colorful anecdotes about my personal experiences or share my own deep musings about the nature of sex and love and death even though my professor had modeled that very well,

14

and had made me thoughtful and adult as his audience. I also couldn't keep my workshops running as long as he did . . . My mentor taught as a confidante—the conference space being fluid, eternal, and open to disclosure of all sorts from students—and I couldn't be this kind of confidante. (79)

If, as Wendy Bishop writes in *Teaching Lives*, "writing captured" her (219), the way it captures most of us who persist, the first main challenge in teaching is learning to translate that captivation. For Wendy, it was doctoral work in composition theory that helped her understand her writing and through it, her teaching as well; for me, it was critical theory. But the process was astonishingly similar as we sought to come to terms with a private life of writing in the context of an academic culture that worked, in many ways, to deny our own experience both of self and work.

We began, or I did, by rejecting wholesale much of what had gone into my early academic preparation before I began Ph.D. study and learned to reframe my thinking, both in general and particular, with regard to what it was I thought I was doing when I was writing. If the men who taught as confidantes had done little to shape my experience of writing beyond the narrative of their own writing lives, I would have nothing to do with their methods. I would observe strict boundaries and proper professional decorum, rejecting the concept of mentoring altogether and embracing *theory* as a neutral and generative ground. I and others like me were anxious to forge out on our own. Bishop hoped for nothing less than to change her profession; if I'd let myself think this, I'd have wanted it too.

Twenty years later, I look back on this moment of our coming into being in academia as a moment in which we expected that the apparent right-mindedness of our thinking was going to open everything up in a heartbeat. So it's with some frustration that I read Bizzaro's comment (2004) that "the mere mention of *theory* or *praxis* sets off alarms in the brains of most creative writers" (295). And yet, the last time I presented with Bishop at AWP (2002), there were plenty of people in the audience ready to move on. The next time you do this, they urged us, say what the new model for creative writing is going to look like, exactly. It wasn't so much, tell us what to do. It was, ok, we get that, now let's finally go beyond critique and look at where we have gotten to and where we might be headed from here.

Between these two points of view—that nothing or everything has changed—the struggle continues as we seek to convince not just ourselves, but all our English colleagues that what creative writing has to offer in the classroom goes beyond the familiar production of student poems and stories to an enriched experience of the various activities that we engage in, in general, throughout English studies. Bizzaro argues that it's critical to say so, to note what Kelly Ritter calls our "markers of professional difference" (208), lest we be subsumed beneath the still capacious umbrella of literary scholarship. We're not like them, he says, though all of us share a great deal in common. At least part of the time, we need to be looking at how we are different.

Of course we had no way of knowing at that last AWP that there would not be a next time, and that Wendy's untimely death would leave us to sort out the pieces in the absence of her compelling vision. Now, in the mid-career dilemma of self-reflection—on what we knew and what we thought we knew, on what we wanted and what we rejected—it seems impossible not to return to our own origins, which from the vantage point of our own years in the classroom, seem somehow more benign and surely well-intended than they ever did before.

They meant well, the men who were our teachers. Surely they did. How could they not have?

Years ago, when I first agreed to participate in this project, I had in mind another rant about how ill served I had been by the creative writing lore that came to me through my earliest experience in a prestigious west coast program. I'd never been anyone's confidante in the classroom—I'd never ranked high enough on the fiercely competitive hierarchy of the creative writing world. (Not, of course, strictly true—I had my supporters, and they taught me plenty. How to take in what they taught me constitutes the long and complex story of my own writing and teaching life.) But I'd seen plenty of student writers try and fail to form themselves in the image of their teachers who were in no way like themselves. I'd seen the falling into silence that ensued, or the clumsy or imitative texts, the uninspired—the *unnecessary*—writing, and I wanted nothing to do with any of that. I'd formed my own crustacean shell around my practice and stubbornly insisted that we commit ourselves, in our own classrooms, to an examination of what happens in the writing moment to let writing take place. Teach, I said, not craft but the intransitive act that is writing itself, as a primary experience, and the craft will take care of itself. Create the structure within which students can imagine the letting go of thinking. That is how writing works when it is really writing.

I've said that, and I've practiced it, and to a large extent it is the logic that still informs my teaching. But I've never been entirely certain I have anything new to say in the context of this current project, and as I turn, again, at last, to the lore on which I was trained, I find a surprising, if grudging, affection for the essential principles against which I defined my own writing and teaching. In years past, when I was struggling with my classes, Wendy used to counsel me that resistance is an essential part of learning, and as I look back at the thirty years that have passed since I first entered the creative writing world, I am struck by how consistently my ideas and behavior, like those of a two- or a sixteen-year-old (or my own students) stuck in a mode of oppositional identity, have been framed by their resistance to the received ideas of what should count as writing and teaching.

Now, as I enter my third decade of teaching, I'm a bit chastened to acknowledge how indebted I am to teachers and writers before me who must have wrestled with the same problems I have. Maybe we used different language, maybe we even came to wildly different conclusions, but our project is, like mine and Wendy's, astonishingly similar, and the common link is writing, how it shapes us and how it in turn shapes our students.

Because, as it turns out, I teach as a storyteller too. And if the stories I tell on myself are stories of exclusion and of the particular challenge, for me, to find a place or way of being in the creative writing world, if they are meant to align me with my students by suggesting that what we share in common is far more important than what sets us apart, they are nonetheless stories of the writing life that happens to be mine.

So what I'd like to do instead is take a single principle of enduring writing lore—that writers must be readers first—and examine how I think it may have worked both to impede and to enrich our development not just as writers but also as a teachers.

Against Reading

Perhaps a critique of the readers-first principle does not seem entirely wise, for who would dispute that reading serves as a guiding principle of writing? That's the one thing we can all agree on, and to suggest otherwise is nothing short of academic heresy. Reading is the one certain thing that we do and it lies not just at the heart of the discipline, but in its earliest origins as an educational experiment to revitalize the study of literature—reading—from the inside, or the writer's perspective. Reading is our sacred, privileged link to the rest of English studies. And anyway, isn't that why we write—to be read?

Read, read, read, creative writing students are exhorted. First you must read; above all, you must be readers first.

I go to visit the creative writing class of a junior colleague, and three-quarters of the class time is spent discussing a *published author's* story. Student writing itself is cursorily covered in the last fifteen minutes, with a few general comments about what "works" and what does not.

If writing is itself a form of conversation with all prior writing, if it can't even be said to reflect anything other than writing, we must be largely in agreement that students who come to us ill-prepared in their reading need to be whipped into shape. The 2002 NEA study "Reading at Risk" well documents the decline in literary readership, especially among the new generation of college students, and only fuels our determination to convince students that reading is the single most important activity they can engage in as writers and that, whatever reading they may already have done, they are already so far behind those who precede them as to defeat them before they have even begun. As for what students may read on their own—comics, video games, a few underground texts they pass among themselves and under our radar with the kind of subversive passion we may only vaguely recall—we're too busy with our own reading (and writing and grading), never mind our biases, to pay much attention to what that might be or what it may teach us about the world our students live in.

I attended a student reading recently where a young woman read a story in which a protagonist fought her way back to a particular book, frantic to reenter its world, with reading itself a main concern of the story constructed as a compelling and vital act—not just a refuge but a whole way of being in the world. It is always possible to encounter such students in our classrooms, but increasingly, they surprise us, however we may welcome our kinship with them. I have one son who's a reader and another who is not, and they came this way from the beginning, both committed to their own lives of language. If one is expressing his connection through academic scholarship and the other through hip hop, fashion, and other forms of social discourse, they are both becoming fluent in their worlds. But it is still a problem when MFA students more closely resemble my second son than my first, or when a surprising number among them enter programs as neither practiced nor systematic readers.

It's been said that we're training a nation of writers who do not read. I've said it myself. I've wrung my hands and felt bad about it and wondered how, exactly, it is that we've come to this state of affairs in only a few generations. For I, like the girl above, was a reader, one of those bookish kids who hoped for rain so I could stay inside and read all day. Therefore, received lore would have it, I should have come into my writing practice fully prepared to extend what I'd learned from a lifelong immersion in the page.

But it didn't take me long (well, long enough) to understand that a steady diet of eighteenth- and nineteenth-century British novels, American masters, and contemporary American minimalism, then very high in regard, was really not that useful to me from my own writerly perspective. I don't mean to suggest that the reading itself was unimportant—that *would* be heresy. It was for me, as it is for many others, the single most vital thing I did as a writer. But I didn't know how to think about what I was reading. I took it in and what came out was a strangely inchoate blend of styles, traditions, forms, and intents—a failed textual melting pot of my own.

In the early days of the workshop, the material for class was entirely student produced and orally presented, and for years I struggled with the poorly articulated notion of what might count as "good writing" that I internalized from the "successes" of those workshops, trying to mold my writing after them, but having little further guidance beyond the advice to "check out the literary magazines" that might "like what I wrote." I think our teachers assumed we were reading on the side, but we received little or no training in where to find or how to read the kinds of writing we aspired to produce. The ideal text was out there (somewhere), and those who managed to intuit it were destined for workshop success. Later, my own training as a Ph.D. student in the history of the genre I aspired to write was a necessary but not sufficient condition for my writing well in it, and though I left my doctoral program with as good an education in writing as you could get, it would take me years to begin to sort out what that education was going to mean for me as a writer and a teacher.

At first, I reveled in what a friend of mine had once described as a kind of delirium—the incredible post-grad-school freedom, of being able to read whatever I wanted. That was the *best*, my friend had told me—whatever I wanted, anything at all. But then the new dilemma: what did I *want* to read anyway? Having mastered (at least as far as passing my exams was concerned) that master reading list of all reading lists—the Ph.D. prelim—how could I even begin to identify that core desire, my own reading lust? And where could I find it and how would I know it? Bookstores depressed and overwhelmed me; press catalogues, even book reviews, produced that most unpleasant sensation of professional envy. With no one to approve what I was reading now, how would I know if I chose the right books or not? Besides, I was not just a young professor with a four/four teaching load, but a new mother as well. When would I ever find the time?

In those years (at least during winter and summer breaks), I began to indulge in what I would learn to describe as a "totally random reading practice." That was how I'd discovered Jane Bowles after all—on the shelf next to Paul, in the Missoula public library—and that one book discovery had literally transformed my life, landing me in grad school to find out how she did it. What would I discover now that I was once again free to graze without direction, hungry for the kind of reading that would remind me why I woke up every day desperate to find a free moment to write?

My own such reading practice was disorganized, idiosyncratic, and highly generative for years. I became an accomplished grazer, keen for paratext and random sentences that would announce, in arresting ways, *look at me, I am writing. Look at me, you have never seen anything quite like me before.* For a while I read only American women writers, and then for another long time (oh, a decade or so), only works in translation. I worked library, not bookstore, shelves because they were less affected by shelf life, market censorship, and cultural and national boundaries. I immersed myself in the work of well-known writers such as Jose Saramago, Naghuib Mahfouz, Christa Wolf, and W. G. Sebald, but also discovered such writers as Dubravka Ugresic, Martin M. Simecka, and Ricardo Piglia. I responded to cadences and nuances not just of language but also of form, and I found myself thinking about how the aesthetic experience of this reading, even (or especially) in translation, suggested new ways to think about how my own writing might respond to the moment of its own coming into being. Over and over again it was what I had not seen before that sparked my interest as a reading writer. I did not seek to imitate but to respond, to enter the elusive hum between what I was reading and where it might direct me in my own work, moving beyond—ever beyond—what I already knew how to write toward something I could not quite yet imagine, what seemed both possible—and *necessary*—and not.

During this time, I was struggling as a teacher to balance the demands of reading and writing in my own classroom, and coming up perpetually short. I'd order story collections and anthologies for my creative writing classes and somehow never get around to discussing what was in them or resolving the ambivalence I felt about their role in my classroom. It wasn't just a question of how to pick and choose, or of proportionality, a balance of time but *every-thing else* that inhered in the choices I made. For if there was one thing we could take from then-raging canon debates, it was that every text displaced another. If I "taught" a story by Grace Paley, it meant I was not teaching one by Jane Bowles (or Joyce, or Ray Carver, or Philip K. Dick). And what did it "mean" to teach it anyway? With habits well developed in their literature classes, students wanted—always wanted—to do interpretation and were amazingly comfortable (much more so than I) discussing the "aboutness" of texts. But when I tried to interest them in how a text was made—the artifact and very thing they aspired to produce—they grew alternately frustrated and resistant. That was not why they read, they said, nor why they wrote. Why was I doing this to them? Forced to choose, I found I could not choose. More, it seemed choosing itself was irresolvably vexed.

Then, at the 1989 AWP conference, I found myself struck by the lament of a mid-career teacher. "But how," he worried, "can I teach if I can't nurture my students on the same great writers who nurtured me in my development as a writer?"

At the time, I was outraged. His "great writers" were the very writers who had worked to silence me and others like me, and his inability to see so was part and parcel, I believed, of the myopic vision that prevailed in the discipline. Now, all these many years later, I'm led to make the following observations about the role of reading in a creative writing education.

Writers may be readers first but, especially in a literary culture that is quickly transforming itself—moving beyond print or haplessly competing with other forms of narrative more immediate and gratifying—what it means to read and what it means to produce language-based narrative is itself a critical subject for analysis and close reflection. Thus, to the extent that we continue to proceed by presenting unproblematized literary models in our classrooms as a primary teaching strategy, we will work toward reinforcing already anachronistic twentieth century views of what counts as writing.

It's not the particular text itself but the problem of the text that will illuminate writing for our students. Curiously, this remains the single sacrosanct element of our profession. Aren't we, after all, training students to read us? It's not polite to say so, but if not them, who?

Maybe Professor A will teach the recent Pushcart Prize book, while professor B will teach only writers from the *New Yorker*, and Professor C, his old graduate school buddies, only those under thirty or included in the newest multi-cultural anthologies, or *Granta*s, or *Paris Review*s. Students who emerge from such workshops, as I did years ago, will have internalized some vague notion about what contemporary writing is supposed to look like, and in the best tradition of imitative pedagogies, will try to produce it. And this is precisely how we have earned our reputation for an MFA-homogenized literature in what Patrick Bizzaro describes as a ". . . workshop-writing phe-nomenon [that] no doubt works vertically, where sameness is passed from teacher to student who, in turn, becomes a teacher who passes certain literary biases to yet another generation of students" (305).

Between the one extreme and the other lies the creative writing classroom where reading as a practice is examined, not just in relation to the particular text—asking what it is, exactly, this writer might be doing, to what effect, and how—that is, questions about *how* to read—but also in relation to larger ques-tions of reading. It's not enough to assert that writers are readers first, or even to supply exhaustive models or extensive bibliographies. All such work serves to reinforce the choices of the teacher and hence the perpetuation of his or her aesthetic biases, and while it can be argued that this is exactly what teaching should consist of, it seems that we better serve our students when we teach, in addition, the dilemma itself, what it means to choose, and train them, as we trained ourselves, in developing their own reading strategies that work to enrich and challenge their writing proclivities and interests.

A classroom model that adopts this practice in creative writing is one that frames the larger problem of reading in the context of the questions Foucault poses in "What Is an Author?"—"What are the modes of existence of the dis-course? Where has it been used, how can it circulate, and who can appropriate it for himself? What are the places in it where there is room for possible sub-jects? Who can assume these various subject-functions?"(160). It asks that students not just read, but that they think critically about their reading prac-tice, that they learn to identify the kinds of literatures that "speak" to them, that they develop their own bibliographies, and that they articulate the aes-thetic principles that underlie these lists as a first, important step in framing and articulating a sense of their own poetics, which, as Rachel Blau DuPlessis reminds us, "gives permission to continue" (156). In asking them to do this, we are training them not just to read but also to read as writers.

This reading is both the same and not the same as the kind of reading other readers practice, and is distinguished, at least in part, by what Bizzaro describes as the ability to read "a wide variety of kinds of texts, from the lit-erary texts we study to gather information about technique, to various other texts of the world, the kinds of texts that not only enable us to gather material for our writings, but also to devise descriptions of what we have observed in groups we have entered" (301). These are the kinds of specialized skills that will enable students to develop lifelong reading and research habits that will shift and respond as they evolve as writers, but they are not instinctive and need to be taught.

Thus, we should encourage students not just to read, but to look beyond the lure of the idealized text, of any one form of reading/writing as privileged over another. We should expect them to become aware of the pressures—trends, market censorship, literary traditions, the classroom parameters of taste—that exert themselves on reading/writing, in general, and their own, in particular. We should demand that they question, always, what they have assumed to be true and enduring about reading/writing, and that they understand the principles of selection—or what Foucault would call "limitation and exclusion"—in their own reading and writing choices.

For, it is not so much what we teach creative writing students to read as how that will determine the role reading plays in their writing and lives. Throughout my teaching life I have proceeded with the primary objective of helping students frame the guiding questions that will sustain writing for them throughout their lives. Here I'd like to argue that the same goes for reading, and that for this to happen, the role of reading in the creative writing classroom must itself sometimes be an explicit subject of investigation. I'd further like to argue that this "how" of reading depends heavily on the frameworks theory can provide, but that, even so, the role of theory—however valuable—should not be overestimated. In an *electronic book review* forum on creative writing pedagogy, Marjorie Perloff reflects on the great promise theory once held for creative writing, and as I am prone to do myself, waxes a bit nostalgic for the good old days of high critical theory when the questions that were being pressed were questions about all the big issues—language, authorship, power, writing. And this changed everything at once. So finally, I'd like to argue that the reading *and* writing we teach our students—and the ways we frame it for them—should do just that—change everything at once, and make a life in language not just possible for them, but wholly necessary.

It's been what, thirty years?, since Susan Sontag argued against interpretation, calling for an "erotics" in place of a "hermeneutics" of art. "None of us," she wrote, "can ever retrieve that innocence before all theory when art knew no need to justify itself, when one did not ask of a work of art what it said because one knew (or thought one knew) what it did" (4–5). True enough. But we can long for it, that innocence, and we can teach it—not the innocence, but the desire for it, and the role that desire must play in the act of writing.

It may seem counter-intuitive, but another lens of theory might help us frame this longing as open-ended and ongoing and so enable us to teach, as I have long aspired, not just how to write a *poem* or *story*, but the practice of *writing* itself, which Barthes long ago described as an "intransitive act," the writing of any particular kind of text but writing itself. Throughout my twenty years of teaching, never mind of writing, I have not been dissuaded that this practice makes for stronger, more arresting—more vital—writing than the craft-based lore that continue to cohere at the center of the discipline of creative writing. With this proviso: Theory can lead us to these questions and frameworks, but it cannot substitute for writing (or at least the kind of writing we aim to produce in the creative writing classroom, for theory, like all writing, is a writing of its own), any more than writing can substitute for theory.

The reading lists we provide for our students are our first markers of interpretation, which does not mean that we should not provide them, but that we should provide them in the context of those markers. The question "what books are you teaching?" must be replaced by "why are you teaching what books and how?" Of course this is more difficult to do than to assert. In my own department, for example, as we worked toward revising the department webpage, creative writing faculty suggested the idea of posting an interactive reading list to which to which we could add or subtract titles at will. What a terrific resource this would be, we imagined, for our students—that is, if our "list" could ever make it (it did not) beyond the first few titles and the heated arguments that rapidly ensued.

For a while in English studies it was popular to teach the conflicts. If we couldn't agree among ourselves, we should at least let students in on our dis-agreements. For some, students and teachers included, all this would prove to be too much information. But if we are going to send students out into a world already saturated with narrative in media more instantaneously gratifying and dramatic than language ever can be (for that is the world that is theirs), we should at least begin by having them acknowledge the dilemma and consider what language can do that other media can not. Just reading is a first but not sufficient step in becoming self-aware and deliberate about what they may choose to do on the page and how they hope that page may move out into and through the world that receives it.

As Writing Moves Through the World

In my own classroom praxis, there is never enough time, and given my ambivalence about the kind of behavior I model every time I suggest that we talk about story A or B, I have tended, on the whole, to leave the reading to the others and to focus on discussions of theory and process. For years, I believed that theory would provide the mechanism through which we would be able to frame what writing is and how it is constrained by and moves through the world in such a way as to give our students agency in it. I still think it can do this, but I am mystified at what it sometimes does instead. So many writers who embraced the promise of theory have left their origins in writing far behind, and as they begin to look more like theorists instead, it's hard not to rue the impossibility of innocence, at least in our relations with the blank page.

Between Bizzaro's powerful throng of conservative writers and the powerful throng of academics some of us seek to align ourselves with lies the middle ground of writing where what has happened to all that promise can still be constructed as a way of locating ourselves and our writing in the particular moment of history and culture that turns out to be our own. Like Marjorie Perloff, I believe that we have reached a point where current theory in English studies, increasingly discipline bound, no longer holds the transformative power of the great shifts in thinking that occurred at the end of the prior cen-tury. Perhaps it is time to take what we have learned from those shifts and, moving forward toward what John Barth once called "the next best thing," reexamine both our reading and writing practices, and how we think about them. We can't do this without foregrounding the problem of what it means to write in the world today, and we can't do it either without reading beyond the borders of our country.

During those last years of that century, in the round, middle part of the nineties, I found myself at a Linda Nochlin talk, moved by her observation that "nothing is more interesting, more poignant, or more difficult to seize than the intersection between self and history." Shortly after that I began to require that students keep a "fact of the week" journal, utterly convinced that though many seemed dispassionate about, even uninterested in, the broader world, it would take little more than a glance to awaken their latent curiosities and vital sense of connection with the Bahktin has called the "open-ended present." But in the relative stability of post-earthquake, post-uprising LA, my students were generally confounded by the assignment and had trouble finding even one fact in the whole world to command their attention and interest each week.

Today, that world is a vexed and altered one, and though it may not be the job of the creative writing teacher to tell the students how to think about that world, surely it should be to expect them to look at—to "read"—it. And as they do, they should ask hard questions about the role of writing in the particular world that turns out to be theirs, and how they would have their own work engage and move through it, defining their own intersection with history and what they would have their writing to both *be* and *do* in it.

This is at least in part why we need to look beyond nationalities to the way writers all over the world are facing this challenge, and why we should encourage our students to imagine their writing as entering a transnational discourse. I don't mean to suggest that we should not, also, insist that students read closer to home, but for me there is something generative, and too often overlooked, about the intersection between the local and the global that we should ask students, at the very least, to consider. To do this, we need to teach strategies for reading and for reading the strategies, as well as, as always, of course, selected texts.

Instead, for the most part, we're still training students to read and emulate contemporary American writers, still asserting the vertical influence of taste that can only ultimately prove to be dead-ended. The craft-based, text-centered, publication-oriented creative writing pedagogies modeled after the Iowa Writers' workshop have much to recommend them, not the least of which is the often gorgeous writing they produce. But if the creative writing classroom persists in certain ways as provincial, the challenge of the writer in the world has expanded exponentially.

In my second decade of teaching, a point came, I imagine, though I can never exactly fix it, when things began to shift, both inside creative writing and within the larger discipline of English studies where it began to seem as though we'd all grown a bit less daring in our thinking and practice. But even while the disciplines came together to form the constellation now known as English Studies, a strange thing was happening in creative writing. At some point, we reached—we could not not reach—a point of critical mass, where even the most conservative among us could no longer pretend that our shared and primary goal was to produce writers who publish and *teach*. Dana Gioia's recent analysis of poetry beyond print culture, "Disappearing Ink," well documents the vigorousness with which many in the creative writing world are leaving academia behind. And while that is, in many respects, cause for celebration, we must also carefully consider its implications before our own institutional practice renders us so hopelessly anachronistic as to be reduced to a footnote of a larger, revitalized literary culture in America.

But the world that once provided its writers a gracious and accommodating home has also changed. Ever more specialized, each of the disparate strands that constitute English studies has worked systematically throughout the last couple of decades to distinguish itself by those "markers of professional difference" Ritter describes. Increasingly, in literature classes, what we see is not the study of literature but the study of literary scholarship. And even as I lamented certain movements on the part of creative writing toward homogeneity and the privileging of any one particular kind of text over another, theorists were busy concocting their own version of McTheories, screwing their lenses ever closer and tighter to produce such professional myopia as to make at least some of us wonder why we ever looked to them for answers in the first place. There are complex institutional reasons for this too myriad to broach here, but one sad fallout is that we have passed the point where the easy commingling and cross-fertilization of discourses and disciplines inside English studies, which theory might once have enabled, can occur. Though in some ways it may seem that our work is more complex and specialized, it is also impoverished by our increasing alienations from each other.

Another Little Story

Toward the end of a long day of writing at an artist's retreat one spring, I left my little cottage to walk down to the beach, and after about half a mile, the following sentence came into my head: "As it happened, Rebbecca's feet did not grow, so though in time she turned out to be a very tall woman, her feet remained as small as an infant's, with tiny rosebud toes and nails as thin and translucent as the membranes of eggs."

Well, I liked that sentence, I really did, but when I reached into my pocket for my notepad and pen to write it down, I discovered that I had forgotten— the pen! Sorely disappointed, because I had been looking forward to the beach at the end of the walk, I thought I should go back to write that sentence down, along with the many others that would surely follow. But then I thought: oh, that's all right, I'll just find a pencil. And so I continued walking on, writing in my head—sentence by sentence—the story that was quickly proving itself to be of some compelling interest to me.

Half a mile farther on and some page or so into my story, I found a pen, but it was out of ink. I looked about the deserted, rural road, the long sweep of it down to the water, and thought: oh, that's all right, it was supposed to be a pencil.

Of course I can tell this story because just before I arrived at the beach that day (as well as at the very furthest limits of my middle-aged powers of memorization), I finally found my pencil, one of the glittery kinds children carry, just the broken-off nub of it really, with the metal at the base of the eraser ragged-edged and rusted, but with enough of the graphite exposed that I could now write down on paper—sentence by sentence—what I'd already written in my head of a story that turned out to be about a mountain climber with tiny feet, which just goes to show that writing, as I always say, is an act of faith, like any other. And really, it's a fine thing if, in the act of writing we give ourselves over entirely to a primary experience of it—its, well, intransitivity, the sentences unfolding in our heads, in the split beyond language where writing takes place and the promise of a pencil out there, somewhere. There's another secret part of me that is convinced that if there's anything of value we can teach our students, it is just that—that writing is an act of faith, that it will be all right, that they will find their pencils, and that writing itself has the power to break everything open and reveal it to us, over and over again.

As a young teacher, I found it very easy to be clear and authoritative (despite my ambivalence and efforts to disrupt the concept of authority itself). I knew, after all, very little, so everything I knew seemed important and worth insisting on. Now, everything I know seems linked to every other thing and it feels increasingly impossible to make any assertion without also allowing for its opposite, and more. I have argued here against received models of reading because I do not believe we can proceed as though reading has an inherent value beyond how it connects us to the ways we have always used language and form to shape and give meaning to experience. Admittedly, that's a lot, but it is reduced to nothing if we begin without marking the paradox itself.

I have argued against reading the same way I might have argued against fix-it paradigms of the creative writing workshop or mentor-model pedagogies organized around the figure of the teacher/writer. In a recent contemporary American literature class, I proceeded from a writerly perspective, convinced that if reading is good for writers, surely writing must be good for readers. The result was, I must admit, mixed, with a good number of students revealing themselves to be closet writers, but with an equally sizeable number wondering openly why I was doing this to them. But at least some among them rediscovered writing—I know, because they told me—as a link to their original pleasure of the text and what it has to teach them about the way we might read not just the text, but also the world of the text and ourselves as a part of that world.

Maybe that's a small thing, but more often than not it's what captures us first. Now, for the rest of our lives, we will be struggling to understand that captivation. We begin with a sentence and a pencil. But first, we must find them both.

Bibliography

Amato, Joe, and H. Kassia Fleisher. "Reforming Creative Writing Pedagogy: History as Knowledge, Knowledge as Activism" Creative Writing Pedgaogy Cluster. *electronic book review*. Accessed 2001: http://www.altx.com/ebr/riposte/rip2/rip2ped/amato.htm. With responses by Sandy Huss, Marjorie Perloff, and David Radavich.

Bishop, Wendy. 1997. *Teaching Lives: Essays and Stories*. Logan, Utah: Utah State University Press.

Bizzaro, Patrick. 2004. "Research and Reflection in English Studies: The Special Case for Creative Writing." *College English* 66.2: 294–309.

DePless, Rachel Blau. 1990. *The Pink Guitar: Writing as Feminist Practice*. New York: Routledge.

Foucault, Michel. 1979. "What Is an Author?" In *Textual Strategies: Perspectives in Post-Structuralist Criticism*. Josue V. Harari, ed. Ithaca: Cornell University Press.

Ritter, Kelly. 2001. "Professional Writers/Writing Professionals: Revamping Teaching Training in PhD Programs." *College English* 64.2: 205–27.

Sontag, Susan. 2001. *Against Interpretation and Other Essays*. New York: Picador.

3

Charming Tyrants and Faceless Facilitators

The Lore of Teaching Identities in Creative Writing

By Mary Ann Cain

For Lil, Judy, Judith, Steve, Toni, and (always) George

"[A] counterstory [is] a narrative that takes up a shared but
oppressive understanding of who someone is and sets out to shift it."
—Hilde Lindemann Nelson,
Damaged Identities, Narrative Repair (69).

I already had a Master's degree in Creative Writing but was on a quest for a
teacher, one who wrote the way I wanted to write, who told the kinds of truths
I was committed to, who had the power and prestige I secretly longed for. Yet
I didn't claim to be on a quest. Instead, I said that I "just wanted time to write"
and "needed some time out" from the eight-to-five university civil service jobs
I'd held since finishing my degree.

What I really wanted was a Mentor. Not a pragmatic, "showing-the-
ropes" kind to guide me on how to publish my work, shine my reputation,
and attract favorable attention and reviews. All that would be a bonus, but
that was not the object of my quest. Instead, I wanted someone to help
explain me to myself. That is, someone who could read my work and say,
"Here's what I think you're trying to do," and then suggest ways to do it better—or do something else. At that time, working on my writing and working
on myself was more or less the same thing to me. I wanted a Mentor who
understood that, who understood what I was up to and could show me how
to keep going. Two years out of graduate school, I didn't think I could keep
going on my own. Like hot house flowers that lose their luster once transported
to a less temperate climate, I found it difficult to sustain a writing life outside
academia.

The writing teachers I'd had in the past, from high school through my M.A., hadn't been Mentors. Maybe they weren't able to be (they were all white, middle-aged men, with the exception of one female graduate teaching assistant, who went on for a Ph.D. and later committed suicide, and a visiting female poetry instructor who left the university after a year); or maybe they didn't think of teaching as mentoring. Instead, they offered "objective" readings of my work, uninfluenced by my intentions or desires. I had learned the Intentional Fallacy as part of my training in literary criticism, so at least I knew they had reasons to teach this way. They didn't ask me what I had in mind, and it didn't occur to me to tell them.

Perhaps it was this objectification of my work/myself that had stirred my post-Master's desire for the opposite: not to see my work/myself through a stranger's eyes (making me even more of a stranger to my work/myself than I already was) but through the eyes of a familiar. If my true abilities and talents were finally "seen" by the "right" person (i.e. Mentor), I would be able to live the writer's life I had often imagined, one less governed by 8 to 5, turning the work on and off on a predetermined schedule, and more by a continual romance with words, images, and ideas.

At that time Famous Author, whose star was rising quickly on the national scene, was the only living writer I knew whose work had claimed my unquestioned respect and admiration. Perhaps one reason I felt my teachers had failed me was because their work had seemed lesser in my eyes: not daring nor righteous enough, with one foot in the lyrical heavens or one in the humus of common ground, but not both at the same time. In contrast, even before Famous Author's star had risen, Famous Author's work was already mythic to me. It didn't hurt that Famous Author lived in the East but was from the Midwest. I, too, was from the Midwest, but was currently living in the West, a place familiar from family vacations and family roots, the setting of my boyfriend-later-husband's boyhood dreams. But I still dreamed of going East, home to the intelligensia, to artists and writers who were otherwise just names on bookstore shelves.

This quest still possessed me when I applied to the doctoral program at Eastern University, where Famous Author held an Endowed Chair. Despite cautions and disclaimers from the graduate director in the English department, stating that Famous Author only taught one class per year and that that class was limited to a few select students, and that my acceptance into the doctoral program was no guarantee that I would ever have a class with Famous Author, I was eager to pack up and leave the admittedly fragile security I'd established with my poet husband in the foothills of the Rockies and move us to a more distant view of much older mountains in the East. I rationalized the risks: It was a time-out from the deadening eight-to-five routine; as a fully funded graduate assistant, I would be *paid* to write. So what if I didn't get a class with Famous Author? But deep down I knew that's why I would go, for the chance. My life was being written by a familiar narrative—risking all for the sake of adventure and romance.

* * *

Myths are the stories that write our lives; they are the cultural narratives we live by. To be a writer, then, is to invoke a peculiar hubris, to act as if one is writing the story, and not the other way around. Educated to embrace this hubris, then, I could have hardly imagined that the story I was scripting for myself at the time was destined for unforeseen conflicts. As feminist literary theorist and poet Rachel Blau DuPlessis has noted, quest and romance narratives have been set into social opposition for women since the 19th century, when middle-class women's contributions to the overall economy were constrained to caring for husband, children, and home. In her analysis of British and American literature of this period, Du Plessis observes that the only permissible endings for women's narratives were either the marriage of the woman (thus firmly enfolding her into the existing social order) or death (by virtue of being outside the status quo). Thus, even as I imagined my life as a writer as both a quest and romance narrative, only two possible resolutions existed: forsaking quest in favor of romance (i.e. "marriage" into the existing social order, which I had already discovered could not sustain my life as a writer); or forsaking romance in favor of quest (which amounted to "death" in terms of foregoing a public "face" as a writer, since a women's quest was, literally and figuratively, "impossible" outside social convention). Ultimately, to make this move, I settled upon an uneasy "resolution"; I claimed my quest as a "time out" from my romance with conventional eight-to-five life, the quest reduced to a private deviation from social expectations, just for "myself."

* * *

My husband and I joined the English department at Eastern University as graduate teaching assistants; I was accepted as a fiction writer, he as a poet. Two weeks after we'd settled into our carriage house apartment, we attended the first meeting for teaching assistants. I expected to be told what books I could use, what syllabi to follow, what policies and procedures with which to comply. When I volunteered a comment about how to correct students' papers, I expected to be seen as serious and responsible. Instead, my statement was met with a question: Why do you want to do that? It wasn't a rhetorical question, i.e. Don't do that. It was a real question. Why *did* I want to correct student papers? I'd never seen it as a choice, but rather an inevitability: You teach composition, you mark errors. End of story. In the question, other possibilities asserted themselves. Memories of my own learning surfaced. No one had ever "corrected" my writing as an undergraduate or graduate student. A random error here and there, yes, but not the extended error hunt I was used to enacting as a teaching assistant in the Master's program.

That question was just the beginning of my introduction to critical terms such as "process approach," "critical pedagogy," "student-centered teaching," as well as critical and feminist theories that, in their questioning of unspoken assumptions about "the way things were," helped prompt me to think about my work/myself in different terms. For instance, I could ask why I had come back to school and what I considered to be my work.Theory gave me language for my questions.

One answer to why I had returned to school was my quest for a Mentor. Once I recognized this quest, I started to doubt that this was the story I wanted to live by and for. Did I want to surrender my work/myself to a Mentor? Could I love someone so much as to forego any critical questioning? My current teachers were teaching me how to raise such questions, and the newfound freedom was intoxicating. This critical questioning of my work/myself and of others beckoned as a new quest.

During my second semester, when I was accepted into Famous Author's class, I had lots of questions about and felt strong resistances to being/becoming like Famous Author, submitting to the hegemony of name and fame that structured the writing world. Furthermore, my acceptance was immediately complicated because Famous Author's class had been scheduled at the same time as a class I was already in, Composition Theory. I had already put several demanding weeks' worth of work into this class and had enjoyed the challenges. Now just because Famous Writer wanted to teach the four-week course of ten "select" students at this time, I was expected to abandon my composition theory course and (most likely) delay my graduation and put myself into debt, all for the honor of four weeks with Famous Author. My quest of risking it all for my longed-for Mentor began to reveal its true perils.

Yet I had already given up so much, risked a steady job, the soul-stirring West, friends, familiarity, to come East. How could I not take this class? I'd always be able to say I had had a class with Famous Author.

But what if Famous Author didn't match up to my ideal? I hadn't thought of surrender as a dark side to this romance. What if I gave in and dropped the composition theory class to sign on with Famous Author? What if Famous Author turned out to be not a sympathetic familiar but a Charming Tyrant who insisted on surrender without question?

I had my doubts. I called the graduate director about the schedule. I assumed that Famous Author had neglected to consult students' schedules before deciding when to meet. The graduate director was sympathetic but doubtful she could be of much help. Famous Author was not a member of the department; obligations to students were Famous Author's call. I then called Famous Author's administrative assistant to explain my dilemma.

"Just drop the other class," she said. As if this was obvious.

I hung up. Famous Author was looking more and more like a Tyrant, and not even a charming one. My critical questioning kicked into gear: Why does everyone assume I should risk so much just to take this class? Even if I did see the irony (I'm not sure that I did then), it didn't matter. I was in the grips of the quest story that had scripted my life. My choices seemed limited: Either surrender to Famous Author's demands (the romance story resolved) or continue the critical questioning as my new quest (ending in the death of my public "face" as a writer).

A day or two later my phone rang.

"Hello, Mary Ann Cain?"

"Yes."

"This is Famous Author."

Silence. Fear and panic swarmed my thoughts.

"I understand you have a scheduling problem."

Of course, *I* have the problem, I thought. I *am* the problem. I was afraid to speak, afraid that, in my anger over being subjected to the tyranny of surrender, I would say something I might later regret. At the same time I was also ashamed yet pleased to be the "problem child." I had garnered Famous Author's attention, at least for the moment.

"Yes, I do. Your course was scheduled after I had already begun another graduate class." I politely used the passive voice, so as not to directly accuse Famous Author of insensitivity.

"My assistant was doing her best to accommodate my schedule. Unfortunately, it's too late to change the day and time."

Now the blame shifted to the assistant. Why hadn't she looked at the *students'* schedules? I was willing to let the assistant take the fall, since Famous Author did not offer to take responsibility. Wasn't that the assistant's job? I was willing to think so.

The romance story told me that I had to surrender, fully and without question, to the Mentor. The Mentor (and in turn, my work/myself) must be the one and only love in my life. It was all or nothing.

But in fact, this was not true any more, if it ever had been. I had other loves, including the comp theory and pedagogy classes where I was learning to question cultural narratives just like this one.

I decided to take the risk of saying this to Famous Author because I no longer believed I could work in total surrender, no matter how charming a tyrant my potential Mentor might be.

"It's just that I'm very involved in my other class right now," I began. "I've put a lot of time and effort into it, and I really don't want to give it up." There, I'd said it: *You're not the one and only.* Now I was the Problem Child par excellence. At least this was a story I was familiar with.

"What would you like to do?" Famous Author asked me. Me! I hadn't expected this. The romance story demanded I choose one love or the other. I had to think fast.

"Maybe I could attend both classes. I could come to your class for the first half and then go to the other for the second." I had no idea what my comp theory professor would say about this, but I went on the hunch that he'd approve. Being in Famous Author's class was an honor that he was unlikely to dismiss.

"I can meet with you for a half an hour before each class in my office," Famous Author offered.

The prospect of sitting alone with Famous Author panicked me. What on earth would we talk about? I tried to imagine a conversation. When I couldn't, I started to doubt Famous Author's intentions. Was Famous Author just trying to placate Problem Child? Would Famous Author resent me for taking up precious time?

"I guess that depends. Are you going to hate me?" I was trying to make a joke, but it sounded more insecure than funny.

Famous Author laughed. Knowingly, I thought, reverting back to the image of Tyrant for a moment. "I don't resent it," Famous Author replied.

Could it be that Famous Author actually did feel some responsibility toward me as a student? Despite my fears of entering into such a conversation, I felt relieved. I had not been forced to surrender to a Charming Tyrant. I had surprised myself in this conversation, and so perhaps I could again, in person.

Several years later, I am telling a version of this story to my friend, a faculty member at Eastern University where I had attended. She was never my teacher, officially, but we sometimes talked about writing, and on occasion, she offered advice that I welcomed and found important. I am now Associate Professor at Midwestern University, a commuter campus for mostly local students. We are talking in front of a conference hotel in the Eastern city where I went to Eastern University, waiting for a cab to take us to a restaurant. My husband and I are here for the writers' conference that our friend has organized.

"That's the problem with the star system," I say. "You're forced to make these horrible choices. The students deserve more."

I go on to say how glad I am that Eastern University did not (except for Famous Author and the Famous Authors Reading Series) subject students to a star system, how hard I, as a teacher, work to be more of a Faceless Facilitator and less of a Charming Tyrant. Then the phrase, "how hard I work" brings on a sudden drain in energy, as if a plug has been pulled. I picture faceless students with crossed arms, a sign of their resistance to my "invitations" to work collaboratively, to write and revise with each other (and me) as readers and respondents.

"But you took the class with Famous Author because you wanted to know what Famous Author had to say," my friend replies.

I tell myself, I've rewritten that master narrative. I no longer want to become Famous Author. No Charming Tyrant, no matter how enigmatic or influential, was worth giving up critical questioning.

Sullen, anonymous student faces float before me, ghostly quiet in the midst of the car horns and squealing brakes in Eastern City. My students still clung to the Charming Tyrant myth; my work/myself was to show them how to resist that story with their own counterstories. By being a Faceless Facilitator, I could assist in making their faces, voices, words more familiar to them, just as I had wanted to know my own work/myself more intimately. But standing out there in the cold, in a setting both familiar yet strange—once a resident, now a tourist in a downtown hotel of Eastern City—I felt the truth of my friend's statement. Whether or not my students still wanted a Charming Tyrant, I couldn't know for certain, but my friend's words had prompted my recognition that I, in my facelessness, had actually become a Not-So-Charming Tyrant to them.

* * *

In *What Our Speech Disrupts: Feminism and Creative Writing Studies*, Katharine Haake writes, "In the beginning I [located] one fundamental schism between writer-artists and writer-(artist) teachers. I thought of the former sometimes as mini-Shakespeares, and of the latter as dedicated worker-bee types" (4). Haake goes on to describe the tensions she felt when her own "worker-bee" identity was shaken as a new colleague who taught radical poetics in a "prescriptive" way captured the "attention and affection of her students" (5). This tension not only made Haake jealous, but left her feeling unsettled and anxious about her jealousy.

After eight years of teaching, I was struggling within these very contradictions. In embracing the critical questioning quest, I had sought to critique the figure of the Charming Tyrant (in other words, the mini-Shakespeares that writers were supposed to want to become) that had so powerfully shaped my choices as a woman writer. But to continue this quest, I had to sacrifice my place in the conventional social order of the writing world, to give up my public "face" and become a "worker bee." Like Haake, I thought this sacrifice was important for my students so that they would not suffer the same either/or choices that I had in becoming a writer. What I didn't realize in becoming a "worker bee" or, in other words, a Faceless Facilitator, following the kind of quest written by male teachers such as Peter Elbow in *Writing Without Teachers* and Ira Shor in *Critical Teaching and Everyday Life*, was that I had not changed the ending of the woman's quest story. I was "dead" to the social order that my students lived within.

* * *

My memories of Famous Author's class include little about the other students, of whom I can name only three. I do not recall what they said about my work or what I may have offered about theirs. I do remember that Famous Author did not allow us to bring copies or read other students' work in advance. Famous Author insisted that we use our ears rather than our eyes to take in the work. I remember how difficult I found this and yet how valuable. I remember Famous Author being called away during the first class by administrators in suits, bearing armloads of long-stemmed red roses, a tribute to

Famous Author's recent Pulitzer Prize, and how Famous Author, after a polite but brief chat, reentered the classroom, laid the roses aside, and picked up where she had left off. I remember Famous Author talking about control and surrender to the work, comparing the writer to the director of a play, dealing with characters who, like actors, had their own ideas about how the story should go, but who ultimately had to answer to the writer as the one in charge of the script. I remember advice about agents and editors, and how to market a novel. I remember sitting in Famous Author's well-appointed inner office, in an upholstered chair, facing the mahogany carved desk and wing-backed chair Famous Author sat in, eavesdropping on a long-distance telephone conversation Famous Author was having with another, equally Famous Author. I remember feeling both irritated at having my precious half-hour eaten up by this phone call and utterly fascinated by the conversation, especially when Famous Author called the other Famous Author "girl" and used a nickname that indicated friendship of more than a professional kind. I remember when the day came for Famous Author to spend an hour with me to discuss my novel manuscript, the red marks I swore I'd never make on any student paper ever again slashed across inelegant sentences and imprecise descriptions. I remember my inability to take notes, fearful I'd seem somehow disrespectful but also wanting to use my ears more than my eyes for a change. Later, I remember sitting in the institutionally bland cafeteria of Eastern University, watching my blue ink blur into grey pools as tears splashed onto the notes I was writing. I remember the pain of hearing how Famous Author had so thoroughly entered my story, telling of its possibilities, possibilities which also spoke of its current failures. I remember thinking, I love this story she is imagining with me, but I don't have the guts to write it.

* * *

And as the cab pulls up to the wind-whipped entry of the conference hotel, and the doorman in his fancy epauletted coat snaps the cab door open, I know it's no accident that my students are faceless in my fears.

"I thought that's what I wanted," I say, once settled into the cab next to my friend.

Beyond the shadows of the hotel's overhanging roof, the usually grungy Eastern City sparkles in spring sunshine. All I can think about is, after eight years of teaching, writing, going up for tenure and promotion, and now nearly finished with my first sabbatical, how tired I am, how much a blur my work/myself have become. If my students are faceless, it's because I've become faceless to myself. Perhaps the Faceless Facilitator I'd championed as the counterstory to the Charming Tyrant was just the flip side to Famous Author's story of control and surrender. True, I did not want to be the object of my students' unquestioned reverence and slavish devotion. And yet if I were not to remain "dead" to the social order that my students lived by and though, I needed their respect and recognition—a Face, even it if wasn't one like Famous Author.

Famous Author had extended respect to me not by demanding I become another Famous Author but by retelling my story through a voice both intimate in its attention and yet strange in the powerful imagination that extended what I had already told. Nonetheless, in order to hear Famous Author's words as respectful and not simply another kind of tyranny, I had had to question the story that had brought me to Famous Author in the first place.

"But it scared me to death," I conclude. The cab jerks forward into hilly streets, climbing up out of the Hudson River valley towards the shining skyline of the state capital building ahead.

I can recall nothing in my memories of Famous Author's class that would have enabled such a questioning. Only in my courses on pedagogy, composition and rhetorical theory, critical theory, and feminist praxis did I develop a critical attitude toward the dominant stories that shaped my work/myself as a writer. But I also see how the counterstory of Faceless Facilitator had imposed its own tyranny on me and, in turn, my students, by insisting that I give "my power" as an authority figure "over" to students. No doubt some students read this move as disrespectful, since I still ultimately exercised the power of grading, curriculum, and deadlines. "Giving power" in a sense was a way of concealing power more thoroughly except, perhaps, to students most like myself—white, middle-class, female. And it was disrespectful to myself, hiding the fact that I had a "face," i.e. a viewpoint, and was exercising it in the ways I ran the class. Furthermore, white male students often challenged me for the contradictions they no doubt perceived, between Faceless Facilitator-cum-mother-nurturer and Not-So-Charming Tyrant who "dictated" collaboration and collective work. Even though I wrote, published my work, faced writing problems and challenges, I rarely discussed them, opting to focus more on a "student-centered" classroom, when the truth was that I was afraid of showing who I really was, for fear of being labeled, anything from "artsy-fartsy" to "femi-nazi" to "not a real writer" to "spaced out" to "unintelligent" to "crazy." Better not to show a face than risk being labeled.

Of course, the labels were there no matter what. The master narrative had written this ending of facelessness for me—a white middle class woman of the 20th century, on a quest for love and adventure.

* * *

Is it possible to write beyond the contradictions of romance versus quest in women's stories/lives? Can women write/live a story that does not suppress one story in favor of the other? Rachel Blau DuPlessis offers this possibility: "A critique of the ideologies implied in plots always involves some critical response to the rules of the world, since narrative structures are saturated in these rules. Such a critique can involve the visualization of the world as it could be" (179).

I think of Kate Haake and what she has already done to write beyond the ending of the master narratives of writing with her students/herself.

Kate,

Rachel Blau DuPlessis offers hope in a new kind of fiction in which a "collective protagonist . . . replace[s] individual heroes or sealed couples with groups, which have a sense of purpose and identity, and whose growth occurs in mutual collaboration" (179). I see your work and you in this way, as part of a struggle I face within and against my students, within and against the hegemony of the writing world, as something to which I must navigate through both control and surrender. Toi Derricote tells our counterstory, a future written beyond the ending, this way:

Combining our voices here, finding this harmony of purpose—in spite of vast and excruciating separations between us (my primal "self" and "other")—is a revision of the creative act itself, not as an individual attainment but a dialogue of diverse voices, whose held complexities *are* resolution—perhaps even healing—are form. (22)

Bibliography

Derricote, Toi. 1997. *The Black Notebooks*. New York: Norton.

DuPlessis, Rachel Blau. 1985. *Writing Beyond the Ending: Narrative Strategies of Twentieth-Century Women Writers*. Bloomington, IN: Indiana University Press.

Elbow, Peter. 1973. *Writing Without Teachers*. New York, Oxford University Press.

Haake, Katharine. 2000. *What Our Speech Disrupts: Feminism and Creative Writing Studies*. Urbana, IL: NCTE Press.

Nelson, Hilde Lindemann. 2001. *Damaged Identities, Narrative Repair*. Ithaca, NY: Cornell University Press, 2001.

Shor, Ira. 1987. *Critical Teaching and Everyday Life*. Chicago: University of Chicago Press.

4

"A Better Time Teaching"

A Dialogue About Pedagogy and the Antioch-LA MFA

By David Starkey and Eloise Klein Healy

David Starkey: In the past, instruction in pedagogy has not normally been a part of MFA in creative writing programs. If they were lucky enough to find jobs, graduate student writers were basically expected to mimic the behavior of their teachers, but they were not taught how to teach. The emphasis has always been on improving one's own writing.

Of course that's a main focus of the low-residency MFA at Antioch-Los Angeles, but as the founder and the first chair, Eloise, you also made pedagogy a crucial element of the program. There are required pedagogy seminars, and after completing their MFAs students can come back and spend an entire semester studying pedagogy. The "pedagogy semester" requires completing and annotating an extensive reading list, teaching a class, keeping a teaching journal, and writing a seminar paper. Can you begin by describing the MFA at Antioch, then talk about how the pedagogy track fits into the program overall?

Eloise Klein Healy: The MFA in Creative Writing Program at Antioch University Los Angeles is like many low-residency programs in that the structure has to comply with the demands of accrediting bodies—certain number of days of instruction, etc., so our students come to LA twice a year for a ten-day Residency. While they're here, they attend lectures by faculty and guest artists, seminars by graduating seniors, writing workshops (both traditional and non-traditional), orientations to required segments of the curriculum, and readings by faculty, guests, and graduating seniors.

There are a number of things that really set the Antioch program apart from other low-residency programs and traditional programs. Probably the most important one is the commitment to discuss the place of the artist in culture and society. Our students take two required seminars—Arts, Culture &

Society I and II—in which they examine the issues of the relationship of artists to culture and the political realities of the writing life. The Antioch student is required to read and write about what a writer is and does in a culture. In short, Antioch students have to figure out who they are and where they are relative to "power."

DS: And, appropriately, that's one of the goals of writing pedagogy also, to identify the power relationship between teacher and student. We do that really well, I think, because I'll often hear students commenting on how a seminar by this or that teacher could be improved, or why it was particularly successful. By their second residency, our students are effectively critiquing the process of their own education.

EKH: It has always been my feeling that many excellent writers stop writing because they don't know who they are relative to the world in which they live. They don't understand the politics of culture, the mechanisms of production, the subtle and not so subtle barriers to living a creative life in the arts. Part of that is situational—if you live in the USA, you have a different sense of what writing is than if you live in Canada or South Africa. When people have not thought these issues and dynamics through, it can lead to frustrations of the wrong sort. Here's an example I always give—if an African-American lesbian poet counts as a mark of her success getting poems published in *The New Yorker* she is in for a very difficult and disappointing life. Certainly there are opportunities for her to publish in that magazine, but she needs to understand that her path may be fraught with obstacles that are not solely based on her talent and craft. In my experience, students who have not thought things like this through often stop writing because they have a wrong sense of how they fit into the world—they fight the wrong battles and the creative spirit dies.

DS: Teachers face this problem, too—fighting the wrong battles, ending up feeling like they've wasted their time—their lives even—because they didn't accomplish what they wanted. Too often, their goals are unrealistic. And they don't value the real, positive changes they've actually made. I believe that staying current with pedagogy is a powerful hedge against that burn-out because it helps us understand what's possible in the classroom.

EKH: And let's remember that the classroom can be a virtual one. Perhaps the major difference between Antioch and other programs is the on-line component. I built the program to have a vibrant virtual community at its core. One of the problems of low-residency programs is sustaining an engaged community and offering students a bridge to each other and to the program during the long months of the Project Period. Using FirstClass, a conferencing and e-mail software program, we can literally "construct" a town online. We have information sites so students can always access program requirements, forms they need, announcements about jobs or resources for writers. We have private and public conferences that function as virtual classrooms. We have student-sponsored conferences that range from chat rooms to serious discussions of books and aesthetics, a "cafe" where people gossip and gripe, conferences that link geographically "close" students so they can make a face-to-face community if they like (MFA in LA is an example). This part of the program has grown exponentially since we first started up, evolving in ways we could not have anticipated.

DS: And of course pedagogy students internalize the online way of thinking about instruction as they turn to their own teaching. So much of what happens in the traditional classroom involves teachers and students interpreting each other's nonverbal clues. "That look the teacher just gave me: I've gone too far." Or "The students are getting restless and bored: I need to change what I was going to do this period." Online instruction has a different dynamic. Our students are very adept at understanding subtle tonal variations in the writing of a mentor or fellow student. I wish sometimes—as do we all probably—that there was more face-to-face classroom time, but students' complicated personal lives make that impossible. That's one of the reasons they're at Antioch in the first place. One valuable pedagogical model that online conferences provide is the ratio of teacher-to-student input in a class. Students are always at the forefront of the conversation, pushing it in directions *they* find productive; whereas the classroom teacher is inevitably much more dominant and prescriptive.

EKH: That necessary decoding skill is related to our translation requirement. I don't believe any other low-residency program asks this of their students, and we do it not to turn out translators but to give students another way to look at language and language choices, and another way to "see" into a culture.

And since we are Antioch and come from a long line of progressive educators with a deep belief in experiential education, we have a required Field Study. Students plan and design a project that must last from four months to a year, and they are supervised in their work by a professional in that field. Some projects are like internships and have led to jobs (one student who wanted to apprentice herself to a book reviewer is now a weekly reviewer for *The Los Angeles Times*!). Some projects lead to hands-on skills—book making, papermaking, radio interview programs, etc. And, of course, many students do some kind of teaching for their Field Study.

DS: Clearly, the program is already distinctive, even without the pedagogy element. Why did you decide to make pedagogy such an essential part of the MFA?

EKH: I think because of having taught both inside and outside of academia, I wanted a program that would reflect all the "real-world" dynamics involved in learning and teaching about writing. The way one teaches writing in a feminist community center is often very different from how one is expected to teach undergrads, for example. But I have always wondered why such a rigid division existed, why pedagogies weren't more transportable. Secondly, I ran into Kate Haake when I was in the English Department at California State University-Northridge and she introduced me to the concept of engaging in a systematic study of how writing is written. Through her I met Wendy Bishop and her work, and then I met you. So, it was a happy confluence of people and ideas.

DS: The creative writing pedagogy community is a relatively small one, even if its members are scattered all over the country, all over the globe. There's a sense when we get together that we're a slightly beleaguered group—refugees, though from what, I'm not sure. At the pedagogy sessions at the Associated Writing Programs conference, for instance, or at the MFA Special Interest Group at the Conference on College Composition and Communication, I feel a sense of camaraderie with people whose jobs, and life experiences, are otherwise very different from my own. There's clearly a belief among us that those who know pedagogy somehow have a leg up on our fellow creative writing teachers. So how does the pedagogy track distinguish Antioch from other MFA programs?

EKH: Well, we are first of all distinguished from others because we *have* such a track, and we like to inject the idea into our curriculum that we should be aware that pedagogies come from someplace and are marked by where they originate. In a way, this is related to our focus on the place of the artist in society. Pedagogies also come from cultures. Cultures and societies dictate what can be taught and how it can be taught. At Antioch, we like to think that we take these ideas seriously and that we should prepare our students to go into teaching with skills and ways of thinking about their students, themselves as teachers, and the learning community created when they meet.

DS: Which is very different from the MFA program I attended. I'm not entirely certain what their pedagogical assumptions were, but they seemed to have had two core beliefs. One: Getting a full-time teaching job was so difficult that most of us would never have to concern ourselves with pedagogy at all. And two: If we did somehow manage that incredible feat, it would be because we'd become superb writers ourselves. That transformation—from apprentice to master—would also transform us into competent, if not brilliant, teachers. Unfortunately, as every graduate creative writing student knows, that process isn't inevitable. Teachers need to learn how to teach, and that makes me wonder why more programs don't have a track similar to Antioch's.

EKH: I think writing programs don't have such tracks because it is difficult to pull off examining who you are and what you're doing when you teach.

Also, there isn't a "real world" reward for doing this difficult work of examination and invention. Employers don't demand that teachers have this kind of training. Perhaps a teacher or professor might be asked to have some tech skills these days, but perhaps they won't be asked if they can envision something beyond the "Iowa workshop" as a way of critiquing student work. It's interesting to note that over the past week, on the Women Poets Listserve, this very topic has been excitedly discussed and ideas have been pouring in about how to get some new models.

DS: One problem is that, while the workshop is essentially collaborative, students often expect the last word to be the teacher's. She will validate (and correct) what students have said, put her own superior imprimatur on the discussion.

EKH: I think teachers are eager for new ideas, I don't think institutions are. The politics of all of this could be upsetting to institutions. Here's a story that illustrates this. A senior professor at another university was to visit a classroom to evaluate the new teacher. When he came into the room and saw the students working in small groups at tables scattered around the room, he said to the new teacher, "Oh, I'll come back when you're teaching." A simple story, but it illustrates the problem.

DS: Even at Antioch, only eight students to date have spent the time and money on an entire semester devoted to studying pedagogy.[1]

EKH: I suspect that more people don't take the post-grad term because it's an additional expense, and they aren't required to have the Certificate in order to teach. It is a pure luxury! But, I should say, many students who don't take that final term, do take the pedagogy seminars or do complete a Field Study in which they teach.

DS: That idea of spending extra time on teaching as a luxury, even for teachers, is one that, unfortunately, permeates American society. If dedication to pedagogy is so little valued, what's the real-world effect of completing the pedagogy track?

EKH: The real-world effect is that the pedagogy track changes the world for the teacher, and in turn, for the students. When you can get the writing teacher to read and think about the teaching of writing, the classroom becomes a more fluid and interesting place. The teacher is "armed" with strategies and is more open to experimentation and is less fearful about trying to engage the students in their own learning. I know that the eight who have completed the post-graduate term have had solid success. One gained tenure and promotion at Cal State-Northridge and has been directing the writing component in the Pan

---

[1]The number of students taking the pedagogy semester has increased significantly since this conversation took place, in large measure due to increased marketing efforts directed at both Antioch MFA graduates and MFA graduates around the country.

African Studies department. One has been working in the Antioch BA program, and from all reports I've heard, she is really getting a different level of engagement from her writing students. They are more motivated and they want to sign up for all her courses because she is giving them tools they have never had before.

DS: That's solid evidence supporting our intuitive belief that this pedagogy stuff, which ought to help teachers, really does. It also speaks to the fact that good teachers always want to learn more about teaching. We can provide the reading lists, the seminars, but that desire to want to be better is not something you can legislate: it's part of who you are.

I keep alluding to my sense that—I don't want to use the word "pedagogue!—but the pedagogy person is somehow different from the "normal" creative writer. I wonder how being "pedagogy people" affected Kate and Wendy, the first two creative writers to teach pedagogy at Antioch. Were they treated differently by students and fellow teachers because of this classification?

EKH: I think Wendy and Kate had a different situation in that they were also mentors in genres—Kate in fiction and Wendy in poetry. So, they were viewed as writers who also taught about the teaching of writing. Kate was always viewed as presenting students with incredible challenges to ways of thinking and doing. Wendy, too, was seen as infusing her teaching of poetry with these new approaches. Her work with "inventions" was very popular and we soon saw these practices popping up in the seminars of graduating seniors.

In your case we have a different scenario in that you have always been "the pedagogy guy" but you weren't working as a mentor in a genre. Perhaps not the best situation, but something that was demanded by some staffing issues that didn't give us as much flexibility in hiring as I first had in the early days of the program. This probably needs to be rethought.

DS: I've been happy to be part of the program, in whatever capacity. But I know over the past couple of years I've done plenty of thinking about who I am as a writer. When I did a reading of my own poetry last residency, I was introduced largely in terms of the pedagogy I've published. Yet when I'm out in the wider world, I think of myself chiefly as a poet. I know that when I sit down to write, I think first of writing a poem. Reflecting on the process of writing is a secondary activity.

In fact, my situation feels paradigmatic for the creative writer as writing theorist. I have hundreds of journal publications, chapbooks, and so forth, but I don't have a big award-winning book of poetry, so in a sense I'm in the same position as many graduating MFA students who are looking for full-time work. I *do* have my knowledge of how other people have taught writing, yet at times I've felt like a bit of an odd fish at our faculty meetings. Who is this guy? What could he have to tell us about instructing our students? If he knows so much about teaching, why isn't he mentoring a genre?

EKH: I'd like to comment on your experience of being "the pedagogy guy." I think another step we might want to take is to include the faculty in the "pedagogy guy's stuff." By that I mean using some faculty meeting day to have workshops for our own faculty. Most of them came out of programs that did not ask them to do systematic thinking about the teaching of creative writing. I suspect that some of them would jump at the chance to interact with you. Teaching the teachers is an interesting pedagogical strategy and perhaps we need to actualize it.

We may also want to put a track into the pre-MFA work, maybe make the pedagogy track something like a Dual Concentration so that a student spends an extra term doing this work before graduating. Or maybe pedagogy students have to do teaching as their Field Study. Basically, because I was starting a new program and dealing with all the nuts and bolts and politics of that enterprise, I don't think I have had enough time to work out all the kinks of the pedagogy track.

DS: You mentioned earlier that even when you were teaching in different settings, you felt you could transport your pedagogy. Most of our students who are currently interested in pedagogy are *not* teaching in traditional venues, i.e., tenure-track college-level creative writing positions. Instead, they're working in community centers, prisons, teaching homeless children, etc. How can we serve them better? What does the published research in creative writing have to tell these folks?

EKH: I think this fact is the most interesting of all. These folks are working outside of the traditional arenas. Perhaps they are pulled there by their personal goals for what they want to do as teachers; perhaps they can't find jobs in colleges and universities.

DS: Both, from what I gather. It seems to me that a whole new area of creative writing pedagogy needs to open up to address the concerns of, to take just one example, poets in the schools. A teacher will use very different strategies to connect with a third-grade girl or a seventh-grade boy than she would if she were teaching undergraduates. There are plenty of books along the lines of Kenneth Koch's *Wishes, Lies, and Dreams* that provide teachers with effective exercises, but we need more high-level reflection on what's actually going on (and why) in elementary- and secondary-school creative writing instruction.

And that's just a start. There are so many creative writing pedagogies that need to be written. Community-college students, for instance, have different abilities and expectations than students in four-year institutions, who are the focus of most research. Think how useful a collection of essays on the pedagogy of teaching creative writing in prisons would be for those just starting out. Our students at Antioch are in a good position to do this work themselves. They're better read in pedagogy than most creative writing graduate students, and they're out there in the world, instructing all sort of people in all sorts of venues. We should encourage them to write about, and publish, what they've learned.

EKH: I would like to survey those interested in pedagogy to see what the reasons are for *where* they are. That would be a good way to know how to give them the best preparation for what they do. I don't know what the research tells them, so maybe we should first ask them *what* they are doing and what they need. Perhaps this group should be the subject of research!

DS: Great idea. A student in the pedagogy conference wrote me a couple of weeks ago expressing her desire to take full advantage of the pedagogy component so that she could find a full-time creative writing job at a liberal arts college. (She's tired of being exploited as an adjunct composition instructor.) And yet, as I began writing to her, I realized that so much of what gets a person a tenure-track job continues to be creative, rather than academic, publication. That makes sense, of course, and yet why shouldn't publication of a book about teaching creative writing be valued just as much? Or more?

EKH: Let's add that everyone has to balance internal and external rewards. Publishing creative work is certainly beneficial for the writing teacher, and her department may not give a hoot if she publishes anything about "the teaching of creative writing." But I would focus on the longer term and underline the fact that learning enough about your own teaching to be able to write about it can only be positive—for a million reasons, not the least of which is the benefit of learning about your own processes and how to improve them. I am often realizing that some of the best things I've done as a teacher were not things I did with the intention of getting a better job. I did them to make my classroom a better place to be—both for myself and my students. Better jobs did come along, but while I was waiting for them, I had a better time teaching.

5

Both Sides of the Desk

Experiencing Creative Writing Lore as a Student and as a Professor

By Priscila Uppal

When I first arrived at York University in Toronto as an undergraduate in the fall of 1993, I knew I wanted to complete a double-major in Creative Writing and English Literature and emerge as a writer. I did not know any "writers" and I had certainly never met one who had "published"; all the authors I'd read were dead. I imagined writers to be industrious and unappreciated human beings who worked diligently to improve humanity by exposing its faults and its triumphs, and as such, writers were only published, if at all, when they were old. No matter. I wanted to learn the craft of writing, read amazing and affecting works of literature, and join a community of other like-minded people in a university program.

But the question of how one can be "taught" creative writing never entered my mind. I assumed my teachers would guide me in the right direction according to my talent, recommend books, and evaluate my work in line with universally accepted standards. Considering how naïve the expectations of my eighteen-year old mind seem now, I am surprised to write that these lore-based notions about teaching creative writing have not been altogether dismissed during the past ten years, as I have hurdled, four books later, to the other side of the desk as a professor of Creative Writing at the very same York University. Although I now know firsthand that writers live, breathe, pay their rent (or not), and even publish before the emergence of grey hairs, I am still convinced that the study of creative writing ought to be interdisciplinary in approach and uphold a literary vision that advocates engagement and involvement in the issues of one's own time and one's own communities. Creative writing should exhibit an appreciation and dedication to the discipline of the writing craft, rather than operate in a self-expressive, internalized vacuum. I thus propose here to isolate features of the creative writing workshop and its lore that contribute to the development of a writer and/or a critically thinking reader.

The Workshop and Its Contents

A creative writing "workshop" course is not simply a place where student writing is brought into the class and critiqued in a round-table discussion. Although this format is an integral part of the creative writing classroom, it need not exist as the sole form of a writer's education. Rather, creative writing pedagogy can be understood, as R. M. Berry suggests, as "a theory of literature" (58). As Wendy Bishop states, a new school of creative writing pedagogy advocates the model of "transactional creative writing workshops," defined as "workshops that keep writers in motion. Such workshops allow students to understand and develop texts within contexts"(*Released into Language* 14). Or, as one of my own creative-writing mentors states, the task of a teacher of creative writing "is essentially a transformative one: to help students connect to silence as a place for thought and for the tensions that can produce art . . . creative writing teachers can be agents of transformation"(Teleky 214). Bishop's and Teleky's terms, *transactional*, and *transformative*, respectively, stress that knowledge about craft and the cultivation of imagination are *processes* rather than *products*. They also reinforce the importance of *active* rather than *passive* learning while underscoring the idea that *creativity* is a *movement* rather than an *end*. The flexibility, adaptability, and invention of the imagination that constructs works of art must also be used to construct a positive and beneficial classroom dynamic. The traditional workshop-only format is too rigid and limiting to allow for the experimentation, multiplicity of voice, and response. What is needed is a creative writing classroom that is truly creative.

While our students might at first resist the intersection of literary writing theory and reading theory into the creative writing classroom, partially due to the lore of the field, which asserts that such theory is inapplicable, its inclusion is crucial for the developing writer. As Maxine Clair points out, "on the whole, students enter creative writing courses without relevant reading and writing skills" (239). Robert Harlow reinforces this statement when he comments, "few of the students—however much they have read—know how to read. And none of them knows how to read for craft" (40). Many prospective students tend to read stories and poems solely for information, as one would peruse a newspaper. They resist ambiguity of any sort and pay little if any attention to the style or crafting of language. In fact, once such writers are addressed as "readers," they will likely resist the definition as somehow beneath their aims as a writer. However, as Nigel Hall advises regarding the development of authorship in children, "It is important to think of young children not as peo-

ple who cannot be authors, but as people who have had little experience of
being authors. . . The result of [this] limited experience is, inevitably, a
restricted range of responses to the demands of authorship" (xiii).

If students arrive with limited experience and a restricted range of responses
to authorship, the task of the creative writing teacher first and foremost must be
to give them exercises that *expand and open* their creativity. Too often my experience as an undergraduate student was structurally and contextually constrained
in the classroom rather than transformed. In a strictly workshop-based model of
creative writing, we wrote, photocopied, and discussed. Rarely were we introduced to theories of creativity and literature, historical or political artistic movements, or competing traditions. The model is troublesome because it encourages
faulty impressions of art and the artistic process. Such a model does not introduce or expose the student to the ways in which art has been conceived, debated,
judged, or experienced over time. Neither does it offer students adequate writing
models or an understanding of the various stages through which works of art
pass before being introduced to an audience.

Over the last few years, the Creative Writing Program at York University
has sought to counteract these oversights by incorporating a lecture component into its Introduction to Creative Writing (a second-year-level undergraduate course). Several lectures are delivered by guest writers and speakers, and
there are panel discussions given by writers, editors, and publishers. There are
also in-lecture massive group brainstorming and interactive sessions between
the approximately one hundred students in the course, whereby literary theory
and the study of writing are brought together. For example, in a lecture entitled "Clichés and What You Can Do With Them," students are asked to com-
pile lists of possible topics for poems while they listen to poems by writers as
diverse as William Shakespeare and Erica Jong, writers who have discovered
fruitful subject matter for poetry in the deconstruction or ironic employment
of clichés.

Although York's lecture format might initially seem contradictory to the
current generation of "creative" writers, it follows the philosophy of critics
such as Kevin Brophy, who insists that "if creative writing students are to
maintain a level of sophistication and insecurity important to resisting rigidity
in their approaches to writing, they should be integrated with departments and
courses focusing on literature and cultural studies" (203). At York University,
in order to complete an undergraduate degree in creative writing, it is manda-
tory for students to take various English or Humanities courses in order to
supplement the workshop courses. We are also seriously considering raising
the number of these classes to further establish the study of creative writing as
an interdisciplinary pursuit. In order to increase the range of responses available to student authorship, students must be involved in a program of study
that introduces them to a multitude of possibilities.

To facilitate diversity and multiple approaches to authoring texts, students
are better off working through numerous focused writing exercises that high-

light and expand student writing, rather than concentrating on completing only a few longer pieces. In my third-year poetry workshop, for example, students are expected to produce a poem a week on a particular topic, which essentially requires them to write in various traditional or experimental poetic styles and forms as well as to incorporate diverse subject matter into their repertoire. In addition to the actual assignment headings, such as "You Can't Write a Poem About. . . " poem or "Invention of the Last 50 Years Poem," I include a short description or inquiry that moves the student through some of the most important critical aspects of the assignment in terms of poetic technique and craft, poetic history, and innovation. In addition to these weekly assignments, students workshop any four poems of their choice over the course of the academic year. The success of these weekly assignments can be measured by the increasing number of students choosing to workshop them instead of "free" choice writing assignments. Many students surprise themselves with what they are able to produce within the confines of the assignments, which are flexible enough to encourage individual representations and idiosyncratic voices while suggesting another realm of subject matter that might have remained untapped if left to their own devices.

As Robert Harlow notes, "One cannot teach originality; one can only preach awareness of the conditions which allow originality"(40). As a student, I may have initially resisted the perceived constrictions placed on my "creativity" by such exercises, but eventually I discovered that the exercises produced valuable creative expressions and triggered more poems outside of the workshop as my critical faculties were constantly challenged. Whereas "free-writing" was also encouraged in class, my experience is that it is more difficult for students to write automatically in the classroom without a focus point to guide them. To address this problem, I have produced numerous stacks of "index cards," each acting as a catalyst for the writer by offering a spontaneous title, or setting, or hypothesis for a story or poem. By promoting flexibility, adaptability, innovation, and risk taking in the classroom, I help students learn strategies for producing transformative art.

When creative writing teachers such as Lynn Domina argue that instructors should "recognize content as an issue" and insist on a "model of tolerance" toward a diverse array of artistic creations (34), they are advocating for an atmosphere where creative risk and experimentation are encouraged, where previously marginalized or unrecognized voices can acquire representation and achieve effective expression. Artistic creation ought to always make room for the imaginative, the new, the presently unknown. The creative writing teacher who can "only help students write poems that looked good in the workshop"(Green 154) is not fulfilling her responsibility. Donald Hall's "McPoem" syndrome is only possible if workshops are designed so as to produce repetitive and redundant artistic voices. We should take to heart Christopher Beach's sad observation that "it is highly unlikely, for example, that Charles Olson's *Maximus*, Ginsberg's *Howl*, or the blues-inspired poems of Langston Hughes would have been written in a workshop environment" (14).

If this is the case, the fault rests primarily with the instructor. A creative writing teacher must be *active* in the workshop *process* of discovery and exploration, where boundaries are pushed and questioned. S/he must act as a guide to this uncharted territory. For me, this requires challenging students' preconceptions about art and the artistic process; introducing them to competing artistic traditions through required and suggested readings from a variety of eras and nationalities; and prompting a variety of approaches to artistic expression. I want students to understand that writing is a *continuous* activity.

Jane Piirto defines the role of a creative writing teacher in *"My Teeming Brain": Understanding Creative Writers* as someone who is an "expert on teaching people how to make something new"(8). The best material of the entire academic year often comes out of the assignments students would have otherwise avoided. By definition, creative writing teachers should encourage the creation of "new" objects, rather than "accepted" or "acceptable" objects. Jane Piirto reminds us that "until recently the study of creativity was called the study of the imagination"(7); the imagination ought to be stimulated and cultivated rather than solidified at such an early stage in the development of a writer, if ever.

To Mark or Not to Mark;
That Is Oft-times the Only Question

Any significant discussion of creative writing pedagogy must inevitably confront evaluative criteria and methods of assessment, perhaps the most difficult set of decisions the creative writing teacher will make. Although creative writing courses and degrees are offered by academic institutions, as Kevin Brophy notes, "Creativity intersects most forcefully and most problematically with institutional practices at sites of assessment" (219). Brophy asks: "How creative can a student-writer be, who must achieve a certain score out of one hundred?"(16). Unlike academics who receive essays from their students, the creative writing teacher is faced with the prospect of grading material that is understood to be *in-progress* rather than *completed*, *expressed* rather than *argued*. Any creative writing teacher of undergraduate students who insists on "finished" or "final draft" pieces in portfolios submitted at the end of the course is misrepresenting the craft of writing. Students gain nothing by this false pretense. Instead, students ought to be encouraged to think of their writing as representing a certain stage and phase of their writing life, and the body of work as demonstrating their philosophical, social, and/or political concerns, their aesthetic sensibilities, while showcasing the development of their writing skills. Thus a creative writing teacher's methods of assessment must be applied judiciously and consistently to all students and must reflect the *transformative* and *transactional* goals of the creative writing workshop.

As an undergraduate student of creative writing, I experienced a number of different systems of evaluation and grading. In the workshops I took to fulfill my creative writing undergraduate degree (a total of five full-year courses), I rarely received traditional number or letter grades on individual assignments. Required readings, when assigned, were not assessed in any way. Class participation was always included in our grading breakdown and, according to university regulations, could not exceed 15 percent of the final course grade, but was understood by all students to be a significant factor in our final mark, likely the difference between a B or an A. In this respect, year-end or even mid-term grades were a surprise to students, as they had not received any indication of their achievement or progress.

Grading individual assignments can be daunting to both teacher and student, as both would generally like to evade committing to paper the difference between a C+ or a B-. To resist applying any kind of grade to student work until course-end, however, seems less a system that benefits creativity and more a strategy of avoidance. In a recent survey, plus a round-table discussion I conducted with twenty-one creative writing majors at the third-year level at York University, methods of grading and evaluation triggered the most lively and passionate discussion. While some students preferred a more flexible and unconventional grading system to guide them through the next stage of revision (such as a plus, minus, or neutral sign to indicate the effectiveness of their assignment at a certain stage of development), others argued vehemently that it was important for each assignment to receive a letter or number grade, because written comments by teachers could be easily misinterpreted. All students expressed the belief that although subjectivity may be a problem, creative writing can be evaluated. At least in my experience, students wish to be graded. However, these students also felt that there must be room for experiments not yielding immediate results. To benefit from the workshop environment, student writing has to be assessed in terms of *progress* rather than *product*. Grades matter to students as an indicator of potential and progress. The latter is of the utmost importance to creative writing as a study, and therefore ought to be considered when determining the methods of evaluation.

Creative writing pedagogy can be understood, as R. M. Berry suggests, as "a theory of literature" (58). Some creative writing teachers adhere too strongly to grading on a continuum of rough draft to final product. This schema has the potential to reward relatively simple and short, though well-crafted pieces at the expense of more complex and ambitious and perhaps less-formulated work. Others are so completely non-committal and uneasy with their role as adjudicator that they too end up shortchanging their students by their own insecurities and, in extreme cases, harming the development of the writers by patronizing them through a pedagogy that borders on infantilism. Judith Harris, for example, recommends a system of "soft grading" (checks and check minuses) along with "a running commentary...[which] includes miniature pictorial symbols such as a traffic light or a racing horse when I want a student to pause or slow down"(198). While Harris's system might seem non-threatening, it represents, conversely, an environment where learning is replaced by back-patting and feel-good, self-esteem boosterism. She continues, "grading is always an imperfect system and should be reinforced by a teacher's continuing prodding of the student's intention"(198). Although I agree that grading practices are not perfectly enclosed self-sustaining systems, Harris's comments signal her own insecurities with the role of teacher in the creative writing classroom; her insistence that the students' intentions ought to be continually taken into consideration suggests a gross misunderstanding of how art is experienced and judged and has likely been undertaken to appease the students for the sake of avoiding conflict.

Group Work vs. Group Therapy

Teaching creative writing comes with its own set of emotional challenges for both student and teacher. While François Camoin, in "The Workshop and Its Discontents"(the article from which I derived my earlier section heading), defines the "Law of the Workshop" as not allowing an author to speak, which he says is "both necessary and terrible" (4), he does not explain why. I agree with him but I believe it is important that creative writing teachers explain the reasons. It is difficult for many student writers to remain silent while their work is being discussed, so I apply this rule to lessen the possibility for angry or emotional outbursts from the author, to keep the discussion *transactional* rather than *defensive*.[1] It is certainly desirable to maintain a supportive and positive atmosphere, but this atmosphere should not be created at any cost. Creative writing teachers are frequently ill-prepared to meet the emotional challenges of the creative writing workshop and often find methods to abdicate responsibility for any potential outburst. The teacher who remains silent during the workshop process, for example, is not acting as a guide or mentor but is shirking responsibility for negative emotions the students allow to surface in response to criticism. Similarly, the teacher who allows students to

---

[1]When Wendy Bishop writes that "students enroll in creative writing courses for many reasons, and they are often surprised at the demands of producing work for imagined and real audiences"(*Released into Language*, 60), she too is beating around the bush regarding a fundamental challenge of the creative writing workshop: Students are often exposing their most private and personal thoughts and experiences to the room and many lack the maturity and/or the objectivity to handle criticism of their "writings" appropriately. Students of, say, Nineteenth-century American Literature may take negative critiques of an essay on Walt Whitman as an affront to their abilities, but rarely as an affront to themselves. Although it is not within the scope of this article to address this issue in depth, I would like to do so at another time, and urge others to continue such a dialogue. The main point I would like to make on the matter here is that teachers of creative writing should not lose sight of the fact that they are responsible for teaching a discipline, a body of knowledge, and sets of skills for effective and innovative communication.

grade their peers in a creative writing workshop is also transferring the onus of blame onto them rather than taking responsibility him/herself.

Many believe that writing is therapy and seek to express themselves without concern for literary forms or revising processes. However, it is our duty as teachers of a theory of literature to, as T. D. Allen writes, "help make students aware of the world, of other human beings, and of relationships between things and people"(18). To expand the range of experience and responses from our students, we need to encourage our students to think critically and to pursue the reading of literature and its creation as an activity of social relevance rather than a narcissistic pursuit.

Beyond the Workshop

Ultimately, the creative writing workshop is not meant to act as a dominant site of literary production but as a supportive and challenging environment for developing writers. As Wendy Bishop reminds us: "the long-term strength of creative writing workshops has always been the audience they provide and the training in criticism and reading"(*Released into Language*, 60). I've always thought that creative writing students ought to be asked to evaluate their course experiences not at the end of term, but after a few years of writing on their own. It is a teacher's goal to create an atmosphere conducive to learning and, in the process, teach students how to continue the learning process once out of the classroom on their own. Creative writing teachers must be responsible for encouraging a wider understanding of art and the role art has played in history, its surviving traditions, and its contemporary sites of conflict and energy. For Christopher Beach to suggest that a creative writing workshop could never produce art the likes of *Howl* or *Maximus* is preemptive. A young Ginsberg or Olson should be able to learn the conditions that allow for originality in a workshop, even if the truly original work of the artist is only undertaken years later. Our courses should not facilitate the lore that assumes the workshop setting creates publishable work. Instead, we should use the classroom to encourage the skills, knowledge, and experimentation within the discipline that might eventually lead to publication. We need to stop *rushing* the movement of artistic creation toward a final product and allow our students to explore the wider joys and challenges of their chosen arts, thereby transforming themselves and the world in the process.

Bibliography

Allen, T. D. 1982. *Writing to Create Ourselves: New Approaches for Teachers, Students, and Writers*. Oklahoma: University of Oklahoma Press.

Beach, Christopher. 1996. "Careers in Creativity: The Poetry Academy in the 1990s." *Western Humanities Review*. 1.1 (Spring): 4–16.

Berry, R. M. 1994. "Theory, Creative Writing, and the Impertinence of History." In *Colors of a Different Horse: Rethinking Creative Writing Theory and Pedagogy*.

Wendy Bishop and Hans Ostrum, eds. Illinois: National Council of Teachers of English.

Bishop, Wendy. 1994. "Crossing the Lines: On Creative Writing Composition and Composing Creative Writing." In *Colors of a Different Horse: Rethinking Creative Writing Theory and Pedagogy.* Wendy Bishop and Hans Ostrum, eds. Illinois: National Council of Teachers of English.

—-. 1990. *Released into Language: Options for Teaching Creative Writing.* Illinois: National Council of Teachers of English.

Brophy, Kevin. 1998. *Creativity: Psychoanalysis, Surrealism and Creative Writing.* Victoria: Melbourne University Press.

Camoin, François. 1994. "The Workshop and Its Discontents." In *Colors of a Different Horse: Rethinking Creative Writing Theory and Pedagogy.* Wendy Bishop and Hans Ostrum, eds. Illinois: National Council of Teachers of English.

Clair, Maxine. 1994. "Oral Literature in the Teaching of Creative Writing." In *Colors of a Different Horse: Rethinking Creative Writing Theory and Pedagogy.* Wendy Bishop and Hans Ostrum, eds. Illinois: National Council of Teachers of English.

Domina, Lynn. 1994. "The Body of My Work Is Not Just a Metaphor." In *Colors of a Different Horse: Rethinking Creative Writing Theory and Pedagogy.* Wendy Bishop and Hans Ostrum, eds. Illinois: National Council of Teachers of English.

Elliott, Gayle. 1994. "Pedagogy in Penumbra: Teaching, Writing, and Feminism in the Fiction Workshop." In *Colors of a Different Horse: Rethinking Creative Writing Theory and Pedagogy.* Wendy Bishop and Hans Ostrum, eds. Illinois: National Council of Teachers of English.

Hall, Nigel. 1989. "Introduction." *Writing with Reason: The Emergence of Authorship in Young Children.* Nigel Hall, ed. London: Hodder and Stoughton.

Harlow, Robert. 1966. "Bastard Bohemia: Creative Writing in the Universities." *Canadian Literature.* 27: 32–43.

Harris, Judith. 2001. "Re-Writing the Subject: Psychoanalytic Approaches to Creative Writing and Composition Pedagogy." *College English.* 64.2 (November): 175–204.

Kendig, Diane. 1994. "It is Ourselves that We Remake: Teaching Creative Writing in Prison." In *Colors of a Different Horse: Rethinking Creative Writing Theory and Pedagogy.* Wendy Bishop and Hans Ostrum, eds. Illinois: National Council of Teachers of English.

Parini, Jay. 1994. "Literary Theory and the Writer." In *Colors of a Different Horse: Rethinking Creative Writing Theory and Pedagogy.* Wendy Bishop and Hans Ostrum, eds. Illinois: National Council of Teachers of English.

Piirto, Jane. 2002. *"My Teeming Brain": Understanding Creative Writers.* New Jersey: Hampton Press, Inc.

Teleky, Richard. 2001. "Entering the Silence: Voice, Ethnicity, and the Pedagogy of Creative Writing." *MELUS.* 26.1: 205–19.

6

Creativity, Caring, and The Easy "A"

Rethinking the Role of Self-Esteem in Creative Writing Pedagogy

By Anna Leahy

In 2002, *Fresh Air* ran an interview with political commentator Bill Maher. When asked why he was friends with Ann Coulter, a vocal conservative, Maher replied that she never pulls a punch and isn't afraid of getting booed a little. While writerly analysis, criticism, and guidance are overt goals of creative writing workshop classrooms, teachers and students alike often deem themselves successful if they don't get *boo*ed. Though a tough-love, football-coach workshop that publicly shreds stories or poems in front of their silent authors is dangerous (as may be Coulter's cultivation of audience ire), so too is a creative writing classroom based covertly on the lore of self-esteem or the myth of the easy "A," both of which can undermine rewarding professional relationships between undergraduate and graduate writers and their mentors. While undercutting another's self-esteem shouldn't occur, teachers and writers must take risks. As novelist George Garret writes, "Without that trust and that risk—nothing. Nothing new or worthy or admirable or ... *true"* (2). When making pedagogical decisions, creative writing teachers must risk a little booing and must guide students to risk being booed too. When teachers and students don't risk contradiction and doubt, we pull punches and trade long-term achievements as writers for fleeting feelings of strength.

Though guidance for teaching creative writing is lacking,[1] our common terminology, the prevalent workshop model, and popular notions of creative writing as unteachable, unacademic, or undisciplined lead to self-esteem as a

---

[1]While some textbooks imply pedagogical approaches, few guides for teaching creative writing at the college and graduate levels exist. *Colors of a Different Horse: Rethinking Creative Writing and Pedagogy,* edited by Wendy Bishop and Hans Olstrom, is an often-cited exception; *Power and Identity in the Creative Writing Classroom: The Authority Project,* edited by Anna Leahy, is one

55

hidden guiding principle in our pedagogy. Consider Jesse Lee Kercheval's introduction to *Building Fiction*, as she recounts her first experience as a creative writing student: "After an opening lecture, the teacher [told a third of the class] to have a short story ready for the next class. I was panic-stricken" (1). Here, well-intentioned but uncritically conceived and loosely planned strategies bring self-esteem, in the form of panic, to the forefront. Consider what it means to posit, "Fiction writers [...] believe themselves somehow abandoned, uncoddled, unloved. They deserve more, understand more, desire more" (Brown 28). Even using the term *writer's block* implies either a self-centered failure or an obstacle that an individual can't name; what if, instead, we used terms such as *writer's shoring up* to emphasize productive pacing of the process? While the writer must remain responsible for the writing process, it is useful pedagogically to look closely at the hidden dynamics of self-esteem in creative writing.

Many students enter math courses knowing that they lack skills or diligence to ace tests, and many take art classes without expecting to paint masterpieces. Creative writing students, however, tend to consider an "A" within easy reach because they have been writing for years and are filled with emotions to express. They come to the course with what Anne Lamott calls "the fantasy of the uninitiated" in which "People tend to look at successful writers [...] and think that they sit down at their desks every morning feeling like a million dollars, feeling great about who they are and how much talent they have and what a great story they have to tell" (quoted in Burroway 16). Our students want to be those writers and seek a place where they can foster that desire. Have they duped themselves? Charles J. Sykes notes in his book *Dumbing Down Our Kids,* "Indeed, [. . .] international studies would suggest that American students not only feel far better about themselves than their foreign counterparts, but that they feel far better about themselves and their abilities than reality might warrant" (49). If so, reinforcing self-esteem may be a mistake, when what we should do is build teaching practices, such as well-guided revision, that reconfigure the role of self-esteem in our classrooms.

Who's Responsible for Self-Esteem?

Most of us who earned both undergraduate and graduate degrees in English and then chose to teach were probably good students who found education challenging, and now want to show creative writing students the wonder and

---

of the most recent additions to the field; and Katherine Haake's *What Our Speech Disrupts: Feminism and Creative Writing Studies* represents a unique theoretical approach. But most writing pedagogy has been codified by composition studies, as evidenced by *Gender and Creative Writing: A Bibliography,* compiled by Susan Hubbard and Gail Stygall; this list is dominated by journals and books devoted to rhetoric and composition.

complexity of language in the hope that they'll figure things out for themselves. We introduce poems, plays, and fiction that will allow students to think complexly about the world and the possibilities of words. However, our good intentions in guiding students can be misinterpreted. Stephen D. Brookfield writes

> Teachers [. . .] expect that students who see themselves freed from the shackles of distorted perceptions and invalid assumptions will feel a sense of release or gratitude toward the teacher who has made this transformative breakthrough possible. [. . .] If teachers are not aware of the strong possibility that students may be angry and resentful [when students' certainty is challenged], they may feel very threatened when this occurs. Under this sense of threat, they may feel that they have failed in their educational efforts. (470)

The things we most value as teachers could be the very things that rattle our students' self-esteem. Their shaken self-esteem can then lead to our own sense of failure. Robert E. Brooke, in *Writing and Sense of Self,* likewise explores the disparity students feel between the role of student to which they have been accustomed and the roles of creative writer, citizen, and critical thinker that our workshops ask of them. In the long run, I think, students become increasingly confident as they face academic challenges and build skills. Yet, in the fury of a particular semester or quarter, some students panic. And panicky students lower teachers' self-esteem.

Negative evaluations, too, can shake us even when countered by positive remarks and when we recognize that standard forms may not assess workshops well. As in Garrison Keillor's Lake Wobegon, at many institutions, the teachers are above average, or, rather, what is defined as average or satisfactory on the evaluation form is below the institutional average. One semester in a previous position, though I was satisfied with above-average evaluations (in terms of raw scores and the institutional average), my department chair advised me that, if I wanted higher scores, I merely needed to convince students that I cared about them even more. Self-esteem that is doled out, it seems, is returned in kind. Certainly, I, like many teachers, revise my courses, but I'm not convinced that higher self-esteem—mine or the students'—should be the goal when adjusting pedagogical approaches.

Very disturbing, therefore, is recent research on attributes of good teachers. Again and again, friendliness and caring are cited as characteristics that students deem most important in teachers. These characteristics seem even more valued in creative writing workshops, where students feel emotionally attached to their work. Writer Robin Hemley supports my conjecture: "The best teachers I've had have always been the most generous, the ones who were willing to forget their own egos and care about their students [. . .]" (53). Janet Burroway, author of a widely used fiction-writing textbook, claims, "The atmosphere of such a group [the college workshop] is intense and personal in a way that other college classes are not; it must be so, since a major text of the course is also the raw efforts of its participants" (xi). In other words, the workshop is built upon *personal* rather than professional relationships; the writing is *raw* effort and, therefore, connected closely with the self; and, importantly, these two assumptions *must be so.* Certainly, I've had a student convey nervousness about having her work discussed by peers, but teachers can redirect a student's fear to a sense of adventure in discovering the why and the what-if that she cannot see on her own; the workshop can be a forward-looking moment in which the student learns to care about the writing.

The larger system, in which creative writing professors are rarely trained to teach in the field,[2] perpetuates an emphasis on caring. In one study of college students, "60% of all best teacher descriptors involved personal characteristics [. . .]. The majority of participant comments (150) could be classified under the first theme, caring and concern for students" (Black and Howard-Jones 5). Numerous guidebooks on college teaching also stress personal characteristics, including caring about students.[3] If we know that students expect or value nurturing, kindness, and interpersonal connections in our workshops and that students are given forms by which to assess our performances, do we accept responsibility for making those students feel good about themselves in hopes that they, in turn, will credit us?

In the prevalent model of "the shopping mall high school," defined in a book by that title, students are consumers, and educators try to meet student demands in order to produce satisfied customers. This model "allows schools to abdicate responsibility for pushing all students to learn and to care about learning" (Powell et al. 310). That is key to my pedagogical concerns: My main goal is for students to care about learning, about creativity and the possibilities of language. The responsibility for making students feel good is

[2]For a cogent discussion of "the lack of attention [...] to the pedagogy of [the] field" (205) and training for creative writing professors, see Kelly Ritter's "Professional Writers/Writing Professionals: Revamping Teacher Training in Creative Writing Ph.D. Programs" (*College English* 64:2 [November 2001] 205-27). Ritter argues that Ph.D. programs offer the possibility for training in creative writing as a scholarly endeavor, as well as an artistic one. My efforts in reconfiguring self-esteem attempt to do what Ritter suggests: configure teaching creative writing as a *"professional endeavor"* (225) in which I am aware of and actively developing approaches.

[3]*A Handbook for College Teaching* by W.R. Miller and Marie F. Miller (Sautee-Nacoochee, GA: PineCrest, 1997) includes a six-page section on personal competency—as opposed to two pages on professional competency—that uses subheadings such as "considerate," "complimentary," and "friendly." The authors claim, "Compliments spur people to increased productivity and satisfaction" (11), thereby reinforcing assumptions about self-esteem. The text also posits friendliness in opposition to "being tough" (11), as if it is more likely bullying than professional distance or worthwhile challenge. Robert Mangan, too, in *147 Practical Tips for Teaching Professors* (Madison, WI: Atwood Publishing, 1990), asserts that "teaching is fundamentally a personal activity" and that a teacher should "[b]e human—in class and outside. Inspire trust in students. Encourage them to express their ideas and opinions and feelings freely" (2). These texts represent a prevalent discourse about college teaching that connects assumptions about self-esteem with what it means to be a professor.

placed on us by cultural assumptions of what creative writing is, by the immediacy of student expectations, and by our profit-conscious institutions. Yet, isn't my attention to forming valuable assignments, fostering lively discussion, and carefully evaluating poems and stories evidence that I care about students as writers? Humility and confidence, after all, can lead to creative accomplishment and informed self-reliance so that students move not only beyond what they already can do but also beyond the need for me.

Creative writing courses, especially those using the workshop model, should teach students to teach themselves. Pulitzer Prize winner Jane Smiley says, "[...] every teacher in every creative writing class has to spend a fair amount of time, sometimes most of her time, showing students how to become teachable, that is, how to listen to what others are saying about their stories and how not to resist but to receive" (244). Our first duty, then, is not to our students' desire to feel good, not to self-esteem, whether ours or theirs. Instead, we must negotiate self-esteem to enrich the writing process of and possibilities for students.

Redefining Self-Esteem

If our students feel positive about themselves, won't they produce more ambitious, livelier poems and stories? Isn't a happy workshop a secure place to share and learn? Who doesn't, after all, want to feel good about oneself and to use those positive feelings to achieve great things? Who doesn't fear that low self-esteem will lead to failure? The idea is that feeling good about oneself leads to confidence necessary for accomplishment. Isn't that what we want for ourselves as teachers and for our creative writing students? Isn't that what our students expect us to create or further?

It is nonetheless worth questioning widespread assumptions about self-esteem as they relate to creative writing pedagogy. According to Lauren Slater in a recent article in the *New York Times Magazine,* several studies indicate that high self-esteem can pose dangers and that low self-esteem doesn't cause society's greatest ills (46). Certainly, it seems logical that someone who feels extraordinarily good about him or herself might be more likely than the person with lower self-esteem to be reckless, disregard the value of others, or turn self-satisfaction into unproductive behavior. In workshops, for instance, egotistical students sometimes attempt to defend their own work or disregard the comments of or, worse, lash out at others. Self-esteem, then, can become a barrier to the exchange of ideas and to ambition and creativity in the writing process.

Moreover, most beginners come to the courses excited about writing but without an understanding of the workshop-style classroom and without strong creative writing skills. Many beginning poets don't yet recognize emerging meter or lingering clichés in their heartfelt lines. Beginning fiction writers often pen slow, exposition-oriented openings and heavy-handed, sentimental endings. For many, revision has never meant more than light editing or running a spell-checker. They want to *fix,* implying flaws, instead of re-envision, which implies potential and looking forward rather than inward. Moreover, even advanced writers find it difficult to put into words what they know about writing. Yet, students seem unaware of their lack of expertise, and the workshop model compounds this phenomenon because it, in Burroway's words, "represents a democratization of both the material for college study and its teaching" (xi). Likewise, Garret asserts, "The special thing about creative writing classes and workshops is that we're all in this together, students and teachers; we're all in the same boat" (4). Everybody has seemingly equal right to, access into, and ability for garnering and disseminating knowledge in the workshop, which is especially inviting in relation to self-esteem.

To question the benefits of self-esteem, though, risks a great deal, particularly for Americans steeped in Emersonian self-reliance, entrepreneurship, and Oprah. "If we were to deconstruct self-esteem, to question its value, we would be, in a sense, questioning who we are, nationally and individually. We would be threatening our self-esteem" (Slater 46). In other words, by questioning the benefits of self-esteem, we risk invalidating those notions that make us feel as good as we do and that make our students want to express themselves in the first place. The focus on the self and measuring its worth, however, as Slater also points out, is culturally constructed.

Because the myths we've made certainly influence creative writing pedagogy, it's worth looking at our assumptions. As Sykes notes, "Quite a number of studies show that students with high levels of achievement generally feel good about themselves, while students who do poorly have a more negative self-image. But here we run into the difference between *correlation* and *causation*" (53). In other words, we've defined self-esteem and its benefits under the assumption that high self-esteem is good. In addition, current notions of self-esteem tend to pose liking oneself as a means to accomplishment, rather than accomplishment as a means to confidence. Slater adds that the higher one's self-esteem, the narrower the range of acceptable criticism, according to one study, so that people with high self-esteem might be at greater risk of threats to their self-esteem (47). It's likely, then, that self-esteem plays a significant role in creative writing classrooms, where students may expect validation, encouragement, and the easy "A." All of this self-esteem boosting, of course, is a version of the Lake Wobegon syndrome in which all our children are above average. Is it fair to boost the egos of creative writers while the work lacks talent, skill, or evidence of effort? *Conceit* is also associated with *self-esteem.* Might humility, as well as self-esteem, assist in the writing process and in building a writing community? If the research is applied to creative writing, building our students' self-esteem may make them less accepting of workshop strategies, less receptive to criticism, and less teachable; we could inadvertently undermine our own best teaching efforts. I, therefore, consider which assignments, activities, and responses are most likely to encourage ambition, build skills, and reveal talent.

One problem that emerges in the shopping-mall high school, which is related to the Lake Wobegon syndrome, is that consumer-students tend to make choices based on immediate self-satisfaction. As well served as they are, "many students—and especially many average students—do not learn. They avoid learning. The accommodations made to hold students and keep the peace permit this option" (Powell et al. 310). Validating self-esteem in creative writing courses placates students and keeps peace; students satisfied with themselves, though, are probably students who don't take risks or delve into the unfamiliar, as exciting and rewarding as we teachers think we make that sound. The strong students probably will learn no matter what, so the emphasis on self-worth could most limit that wide array of roughly average students.

The shopping-mall phenomenon is especially relevant to creative writing because the field is perceived as unacademic. The myths of the creative writing professor include the hard-drinking, passionate Hemingway type or the flaky, disorganized Mother Earth type. We're eccentric, we're free, we're troubled, we're having fun—or so the myths go. These images get us off the hook for professionalism and even position professionalism as antithetical to being a writer. Nancy Kuhl, in her essay "Therapeutic vs. Literary Writing," examines popular images of the writer, including Carrie from *Sex and the City,* and the industry of self-help writing books, including Oprah's role in advocating writing as self-discovery. Kuhl concludes, "As long as the popular connection between writing and self-discovery remains profitable, instructors of creative writing workshops will increasingly face challenges to their authority and to the value of any writing process that incorporates criticism, revision, and audience expectations" (11).

In addition, this Romantic model of inspiration compounds the problem; the author is perceived to lack real effort—writing is not really work—and responsibility for her own poems or stories. Burroway offers a version of this model when she encourages freewriting because "Many writers feel themselves to be *an instrument through which,* rather than a *creator of,* and whether you think of this possibility as humble or holy, it is worth finding out what you say when you aren't monitoring yourself" (5), as if one can and should cease all monitoring, at least temporarily. This model probably appeals to writers most concerned with self-esteem because it doesn't risk the active self in the writing process. The emphasis desired by many students is on spontaneous overflow of emotions, not on tranquil recollection. Talent, after all, is considered a natural, innate ability.

The field itself, moreover, is new to the academy, still defining itself as an intellectual, teachable subject involving skills and choices. As Kelly Daniels notes, the field is a failure if our goal is to produce authors, because only 10 percent of M.F.A. graduates ever publish a book (269). Meanwhile, the popularity of creative writing over the past twenty years has increased enormously. The Association of Writers and Writing Programs boasts hundreds of member institutions, from community colleges to Ph.D.-granting departments.

Some students, now steeped in the shopping-mall model, are attracted to creative writing to have fun and feel good. Teachers probably sense that students who have fun and feel good are more energetic in class discussions and give positive course evaluations, which, in turn, make us feel good and have a direct influence on reviews tied to raises, promotion, and tenure. Self-satisfied creative writing students are good public relations, too, as word gets around about fun-filled, feel-good workshops, perhaps making the field visible within profit-conscious institutions.

We don't seem to know, though, very much about the effects of valuing oneself highly and have just begun to analyze our definitions, assumptions, and goals. As Sykes notes, "A setback that depresses Student B may energize Student C. Researchers have also found that while high performance results in high esteem in some people, the result is not universal. In other words, we really know very little about the interplay between self-esteem and achievement" (54). So, while our intentions are good, we may not need to work so hard to build our own self-esteem or that of our students. Jane M. Healy, in *Endangered Minds,* examines student competencies, low-level objectives, and the role of education in mental development; she asserts that children should work hard in success-oriented environments. Put another way, students today may feel good about themselves and their abilities, even though their abilities are weaker than in years past when objectives were more mentally stimulating. By extension, accomplishment, not self-esteem, could be key even to creative writing pedagogy. In fact, Sykes worries that valuing students and their efforts unconditionally can undermine their trust, motivation, and curiosity. These three qualities serve as foundations for workshops. What benefits are reaped by rewarding students for who they are, what they can already do, or what they desire to do? Challenges and doubt are part of the learning process, particularly for writers; confidence is built by facing those challenges and doubts.

Implications for Reconfiguring Self-Esteem as Teachers

Slater offers self-control as a possible alternative to self-worth. "Ultimately, self-control need not be seen as a constriction; restored to its original meaning, it might be experienced as the kind of practiced prowess an athlete or artist demonstrates" (47). Might creative writing pedagogy, then, be redirected toward providing tools with which students might assess themselves to determine what they're really capable of and to plan ways to expand their capabilities? With this alternative assumption about the self, training and concentration could lead to academic success and creative achievement. Focusing on the task, on the process and the product, rather than on the self, is a better alternative for becoming more successful teachers and students.

Many creative writing teachers model their mentors and accept uncritically certain assignments, workshop strategies, conferencing techniques, approaches to revision, and portfolio models. Considering how each aspect of my courses works in conjunction with self-esteem allows me to actively develop and adjust pedagogical approaches. For instance, "This story is good because I can relate to it" or "This poem can mean anything I want it to" are feel-good comments. Students sometimes criticize published texts when they struggle, are confused, or disagree with the authors' assertions; students sometimes deem texts bad writing if those texts don't make them feel good about themselves. In a workshop, students often want to discuss the writer's intentions. Considering how self-esteem issues motivate the workshop's dynamics helps me understand why and how I need to guide students away from concepts such as intentionality that are more directly related to self-esteem and toward the words on the page and writerly techniques and choices.

In addition, understanding self-esteem has helped me become more comfortable and more effective in guiding students and worry less about curbing their so-called freedom. Many beginning students flounder when they have too many choices, for example, so I now provide more focused writing exercises, writing assignments with guidelines, and more pointed responses. Why not ask all students to begin a story with the same setting or characters so that they can discover their own voices but also recognize prevalent clichés? Why not require all students to write a villanelle, something with clear rules? Why not rewrite a paragraph in a student's story and share that with the class so that they can see what I mean when I talk about wordiness or shifts in point of view? Heavy-handedness in responding to drafts can cause problems if students become dependent or overwhelmed, but I find that rewriting a sentence or rebreaking a line makes a suggestion tangible and opens up options beyond initial intentions. Often, beginning students don't understand our lingo, but when shown, instead of told, what they might do, they set new paths for themselves and understand that they make decisions as writers, that writing is about language.

Exercises and assignments should be distinguished from each other, though, so that exercises don't risk self-esteem, but do foster experimentation and conversation about skills and choices, whereas assignments are critiqued by the teacher or workshop participants. When students use exercises, without re-envisioning, as completed assignments for workshopping, self-esteem emerges as a priority that limits them in their discoveries, in achieving the goals of the course. Revision provides ways for a student to move from relatively risk-free writing to a willingness to risk and to an ability to put self-esteem temporarily aside. As Kuhl asserts, "the role of revision is one of the central differences between the private and public writing processes" (5), and, therefore, offers the opportunity to move the writing beyond the private self. It helps students become more teachable as well, for Smiley asserts, "In revision, even the molding becomes a receptive act" (245). Revision allows students to avoid looking only at themselves for inspiration or creativity; instead, they look to what's already on the page, to something that has become somehow separate and worth listening to. The goal, as Smiley puts it, is for the story to be "now thoroughly yours and yet thoroughly itself" (255). So, emphasis on revision reconfigures self-esteem.

Suggestions for revision, to some students, appear to be harsh criticism of initial ideas and feelings; the very notion that students must revise makes some feel as if they have failed to do an assignment well, as if they are failures themselves. Yet, the portfolio model depends upon revision, and I emphasize revision—as experimentation, exploration, and improvement—because it encourages risk-taking without ignoring self-esteem. Many students resist this emphasis for a few weeks. Students tell me that poems shouldn't be revised because they will no longer represent the intended feelings or that a given story can't be revised because that's the way it happened or the way they want it to happen. However, while revision appears to put students' self-esteem most at risk, students build confidence as they write versions of poems and stories that they didn't know they could, as they move out of complacency and accomplish something that they don't just feel but can see, hear, and share. Revision empowers students when it is an expected, emphasized part of the process. In addition, revision provides evidence of effort, with additional ways beyond literary criteria to evaluate poems and stories, and provides students with ways to reach for the earned "A."

Conclusion: Self-Esteem and Success

Despite the discussion orientation of the course, students shouldn't require social interaction with me to feel as if they are doing well nor should they need an "A" to find value in a course. In talking about the writing workshop, Brooke points out, "Teachers, thus, can only create a situation which *encourages* incorporation of writers' roles; we cannot create situations which *enforce* this response. Learning is in this sense very much a process of the learner, not the teacher" (141). Students, then, must assume responsibility for taking advantage of the context, for ensuring that learning occurs. Moreover, when we see ourselves as responsible for our students' self-worth, we exhibit a kind of hubris; our generous compassion reveals an unreasonable sense of our own power and control that ultimately diminishes students, their achievements, and their empowerment.

If we redefine self-esteem, we can relocate the responsibility for having it: The student who uses the learning process to accomplish goals within an environment the teacher creates is able to build confidence. James Banner and Harold C. Connor's *The Elements of Learning* is one of the few sources to place responsibility for learning almost entirely on the student. Banner and Connor address self-discipline and define good teaching as that which challenges a student within and beyond the classroom. Bill Roorbach offers another version: "To be taught, one must be willing to learn. One must be willing to change, sometimes in fundamental ways, because to learn *is* to change. A writer who really wants to make the next step, to grow, must give up the idea that she's already arrived [...]" (5). Effort is rewarding, anxiety is thrilling, and contentedness is not equivalent to fun. Redefinitions of self-esteem and the realigning of responsibility for self-esteem appeal to me because they fit better with my own experiences, my pedagogical approach, and my understanding of the writing and learning processes.

But I also like to think that, if students work toward building confidence themselves instead of looking to me to validate their self-esteem, they'll accomplish more, figure out and become the people they'd like to be, and even feel good about themselves as writers because of their actual abilities and achievements, their informed self-reliance. Ironically, guiding students as they develop as writers can make self-esteem both beside the point and a positive side effect. If we rethink our assumptions, perhaps too, there will be wider acceptance of various teaching and learning styles. A creative writing professor will be judged within the context of the course she creates; a workshop will neither have to become a therapy group nor be assessed as disorganized by students used to lectures; writing students will gain confidence by making more choices and more informed choices; and teachers will be more confident evaluators. Then, both teachers and students might accept each other's good intentions and also accept responsibility for their professional roles.

A student in a nonfiction class a few years ago came to me with draft after draft. For her final assignment, she wrote about the targeting of college students by credit card companies. She was eager to do the research and, in conversations about her essay, revealed that she was carrying debt because she had fallen into the very traps that she hoped her essay would expose. Her personal experience gave her a powerful writing voice. Yet, her essay tossed ideas around without exploring or linking them well. Finally, during one conference, she burst into tears, saying, "Why don't you like me?" While I had thought that our meetings were productive and that she was ambitiously pursuing important ideas, she perceived my challenges and concerns as an attack on her self-esteem, as getting booed. I explained that I admired the work she was doing. We continued our meetings, but I struggled with how to negotiate self-esteem, mine and hers. I was able to build my own confidence by helping her focus on her text instead of my approval. She thanked me the following term; she felt good about herself because she had developed writing tools that she was confident she could use. Moreover, whether I "liked" her *as a student, as a writer,* probably didn't matter to her any more. If creative writing teachers rethink the role of self-esteem in our classrooms, we ultimately will build a more thoughtful, cohesive pedagogy for this emerging field.

Bibliography

Black, Rhonda S. and Alix Howard-Jones. 2000. "Reflections on Best and Worst Teachers: An Experimental Perspective on Teaching." *Journal of Research and Development in Education* 34:1: 1–13.

Brooke, Robert E. 1991. *Writing and Sense of Self: Identity Negotiation in Writing Workshops.* Urbana: National Council of Teachers.

Brookfield, Stephen D. 1990. *The Skillful Teacher: On Technique, Trust, and Responsiveness in the Classroom.* San Francisco: Jossey-Bass.

Brown, John Gregory. 1999. "Other Bodies, Ourselves: The Mask of Fiction." In *Creating Fiction: Instruction and Insights from the Teachers of the Association Writing Programs.* Julie Checkoway, ed., pp. 28–33. Cincinnati: Story Press.

Burroway, Janet. 2000. *Writing Fiction: A Guide to Narrative Craft.* 5th ed. New York: Longman.

Checkoway, Julie. 1999. *Creating Fiction: Instruction and Insights from the Teachers of the Associated Writing Programs.* Cincinnati: Story Press.

Daniels, Kelly. 2002. "Considerations of Purpose in Creative Writing Programs." *Pedagogy Papers.* Fairfax, VA: Associated Writing Programs.

Garret, George. 1999. "Going to See the Elephant: Our Duty as Storytellers." In Checkoway, *Creating Fiction,* pp. 1–12.

Healy, Jane M. 1990. *Endangered Minds: Why Our Children Don't Think.* New York: Simon and Schuster.

Hemley, Robin. 2000. "Teaching Our Uncertainties." *The Writer's Chronicle* 32:4: 50–53.

Kercheval, Jesse Lee. 1997. *Building Fiction: How to Develop Plot and Structure.* Cincinnati: Story Press.

Kuhl, Nancy. 2005. "Therapeutic vs. Literary Writing." In *Power and Identity in the Creative Writing Classroom.* Anna Leahy, ed., pp. 3–12 Clevedon, UK: Multilingual Matters.

Maher, Bill. 2002. Interview with Terry Gross. *Fresh Air.* National Public Radio. November 7.

Powell, Arthur G., Eleanor Farrar, and David K. Cohen. 1985. *The Shopping Mall High School: Winners and Losers in the Educational Marketplace.* Boston: Houghton Mifflin.

Roorbach, Bill. 1986. *Writing Life Stories: How To Make Memories into Memoirs, Ideas into Essays, and Life into Literature.* Cincinnati: Story Press.

Slater, Lauren. 2002. "The Trouble with Self-Esteem." *New York Times Magazine* 151 (February 3): 44–47.

Smiley, Jane. 1999. "What Stories Teach Their Writers: The Purpose and Practice of Revision." In *Creating Fiction,* J. Checkoway, ed. pp. 244–55. Cincinnati: Story Press.

Sykes, Charles J. 1995. *Dumbing Down Our Kids: Why America's Children Feel Good About Themselves but Can't Read, Write, or Add.* New York: St. Martin's.

7

Writing in Public

Popular Pedagogies of Creative Writing

By Michelle Cross

I would like to propose a simple typology of popular creative writing pedagogy. My goal is to distinguish between some dominant aims and desired outcomes at work in the teaching and learning of creative writing. I am focusing on texts commonly classified under "writing," "creative writing," or "authorship." For each type, I will point to some popular authors or mass-market publications that typify the genre, and then give a cursory glance to the type's stances in relation to certain literary, pedagogical or 'writerly' issues.

These types would for the most part be best referred to as "ideal-types," and the typology itself is a largely symbolic act. While I do believe that many books about creative writing can be linked to these pedagogical types, I'm under no illusions that the types are comprehensive or mutually exclusive, and I recognize that rarely, if ever, would a particular text fit into a single category. My aim here is to initiate exploration into the ways we can shift the dominant focus off of the creative writing classroom or program. These largely bureaucratic and organizational structures within which a dominant mandate may be circulated, cannot possibly operate with consistent or intrinsic ideology, given the number of individual practitioners and students influencing the daily operation of the classroom. Moving away from classroom-centered analysis allows for an untangling of the discursive pedagogical threads that weave together students and teachers on the loom of the classroom.

Two points of clarification. First, by "popular," I am not referring to pedagogies of *popular literature*, such as books about how to write romances, westerns, and "best-sellers"; these pedagogies fall *within* my typology, but for my purposes "popular" pedagogy refers to those discourses about creative writing study that take place in popular or public cultures. The second point may be self-evident in the first half of this essay: by identifying these pedagogies as "popular," I don't mean to imply that they are restricted to these

designations; creative writing classrooms invoke plenty of popular notions
about writing, literature, authorship, etc., so these pedagogical types will likewise have made appearances, whether or not as *types* per se.

Literary Pedagogy

> . . . every novel can be a thoroughly craftsmanlike job, fit to print as
> it stands.
>
> —John Braine, *Writing a Novel* (12)

> My students . . . taught me what they wanted to know. It became
> clear that, apart from time, honesty, and an open mind, what they
> most craved was discipline. Their response to a variety of
> experimental assignments showed me that they were most
> enthusiastic about the rigors of simple craft . . .
>
> —Janet Burroway, *Writing Fiction:*
> *A Guide to Narrative Craft* (xii)

Literary pedagogy focuses on schooling students in what are seen as the basic
elements of the "craft" of literature. Usually these texts focus on a single
genre, as each genre is seen to have unique, specific properties and requirements. In fiction, the canonical elements of study usually consist of plot,
character, setting, conflict, dialogue, point-of-view, and occasionally the more
vague and esoteric categories of 'voice' and 'theme.' Notable authors of fiction pedagogy include John Braine, Janet Burroway, E. M. Forster, and John
Gardner. For poetry, literary pedagogy might cite the traditional 'devices'
analyzed in the literary study of poetry, such as metaphor and simile, but it
would rarely encourage the use of classical rhyme and metric schemes, elements seen as archaic within contemporary literature. Reference is made to
published authors and their works, but typically the focus is on the generic
mechanics of a selected work, and not its topical or thematic concerns, nor
the author's own historical, cultural, or biographical contexts. Literary pedagogy is likely to be reproduced within the other pedagogical types, but its
major distinction from commercial and holistic approaches is that its aim is
to achieve success within a genre or a tradition of literature, on the bases of
style and design; commercial success or authorial self-development are secondary concerns. Its authors may be lesser-known or well-known; in the latter case, the text may or may not function as both literary and iconic pedagogy (see below), depending on how it relates to other works by the author,
or how independently successful it becomes with students. As its tenets are
seen to be based on more enduring or 'essential' aspects of literary practice
than the slippery, lofty pedagogical objectives of self-discovery or commercial ambition, literary pedagogy may be more commonly invoked in the creative writing classroom than other types.

Commercial Pedagogy

> Writers will have to recognize the fact that this is a profession and
> that the carnival, big-book aspects are fast disappearing. A writer
> who wants to become successful will have to face the fact that a
> professional presentation of his work is necessary.
> —Anita Diamant, *The Writer's Handbook* (13)

> If I can take my readers along with me, give them pleasure, and pay
> the rent in the process, I am a contented man.
> —John Stevenson, *Writing Commercial Fiction* (3)

Commercial pedagogy focuses on literary texts in the context of a market-
driven public culture. It implicitly conceives of creative writing as a vocation,
and of the writer as professional labourer engaging in economic activity in an
industry, more so than pursuing a path of artistic or spiritual self-discovery.
As such, the lessons therein may vary in their specific suggestions for the
craft of writing–from codified genre conventions to loose principles of plot
and character development–but are linked in their explicit recognition of the
market as having a palpable presence in and influence on the writer's life and
work. This type came to prominence in the 1970s and 1980s, alongside the
movement of publishers toward "producing mass merchandise for the malls"
(Epstein 105), the modern market success of popular genres, and the
increased celebrity of "name-brand best-selling authors" (Epstein 19).
Observing these trends, many aspiring writers sought out texts that would
streamline their written works for the best chances of commercial success.
This led to a bevy of technical guides and indexes about the writing 'profession.' Indexes of publishers, such as the annual *Writer's Market* directory,
stick to purely practical, technical information for writers, while *The Writer's
Handbook*, *Novel and Short-Story Writer's Market,* and *Fiction Writer's
Market* include essays on 'craft' and interviews with famous authors discussing writing as profession. Writer's Digest titles such as *How You Can
Make Twenty Thousand Dollars a Year Writing: No Matter Where You Live*
(1980), *How to Write Short Stories That Sell* (1980), and *Profitable Part-
Time—Full-Time Freelancing* (1980) are now mostly out-of-print, and not
surprisingly, as the popular taste for generic literature seems to have moved
away from the genres and toward more "midlist" literary endeavors, as found
on Oprah's Book Club, for instance. But titles such as *Writing the Breakout
Novel* (Writer's Digest, 2002) and *The Career Novelist* (Heinemann, 1996),
while less doctrinaire than their precedents, suggest that commercial creative
writing pedagogy is still in demand.

For their part, many working writers and creative writing program faculty
have sought to bury the memory of this pedagogical type in the past, denigrat-
ing any would-be writers who would shape their goals according to mar-
ketability or economic outcomes. Editors and publishers echo this sentiment,

ostensibly in the hopes of improving their own pool of manuscripts. "People who try to figure out what's hot and re-create it are as close to delusional as you can get . . . There comes a time where you have to let go of the New York fantasy in service of just getting on with it" (Lerner 25). But despite its apparent vulgarity, commercial creative writing pedagogy may deserve credit for its lack of illusions, having looked at and engaged with the current literary publishing business for what it is—a profit-oriented industry—and having made the most out of it all the same. The industry has not changed, but has only become more massively corporatized, and the commandment that "thou shalt not be in it for the money" has served publishers better than writers. Arguably, certain holistic, literary, and iconic pedagogical approaches are equally embedded in the same acceptance of market realities. Like the myth of the hardworking immigrant, the fatalistic idea that 'good' literature will transcend the fate of the starving artist and prevail over the market is an attitude that serves to further naturalize the market-driven nature of the industry, and potentially propels unsuspecting aspiring writers into creative writing programs that do not properly credential students for professional survival, let alone success, after graduation.

Holistic Pedagogy

> Natural writing is first of all an act of self-definition of what you
> know, what you discover, what you wonder about, what you feel,
> see, hear, touch, taste—all of which reflects the many-faceted
> crystal that you are. The result of expressing your experience is a
> unique voice: yours.
> —Gabrielle Rico, *Writing the Natural Way* (16)

> One of the main aims in writing practice is to learn and trust your
> own mind and body; to grow patient and nonaggressive. Art lives in
> the Big World. One poem or story doesn't matter one way or the
> other. It's the process of writing and life that matters.
> —Natalie Goldberg, *Writing Down the Bones* (12)

Holistic creative writing pedagogy focuses on engendering a writing experience that contributes to the discovery, development, and healing of the writer's spiritual and emotional *self*, first and foremost. As it values process over product, writing over literature, and individual concerns over social concerns, holistic pedagogy tends to play up the personal and downplay discussions of craft, publication, famous authors, or literary themes. There is often an increased emphasis on the materiality and aesthetics of the writing process—the writing space, the supplies used, and perhaps even the writer's body, as in John Lee's *Writing from the Body* (1994).

This pedagogical type has increased in prevalence alongside the self-help and new-age spirituality movements and markets of the 1990s and early

2000s; a demographic of people Robert C. Fuller labels "spiritual, but not religious" (4), and a flurry of publications that Steven Starker assesses as "a highly visible and powerful force in American society" (1). A holistic approach to creative writing was articulated early on by author Brenda Ueland (*If You Want to Write*), and prominent authors in the genre now include Natalie Goldberg, Julia Cameron, Gabrielle Rico, and, to an extent, Anne Lamott.

Holistic pedagogy has an ambivalent relationship with the creative writing classroom, as a degree-granting program that requires the payment of high tuition fees and the assignment of marks may be more obviously at odds with a process of spiritual self-development than, for instance, a local writer's group. But at the same time, because of their inability to assure students of economic or professional opportunities after graduation, creative writing programs implicitly rely on students to find their own personal motives, often holistic, for enrolling. David Radavich sees creative writing programs as flawed "in their overemphasis on self-expression," with students often "seeking to find themselves, to come to terms with their needs, drives, and identities and to develop a workable means of personal expression" (109). Ironically, though, Radavich "recommend[s] MFA writing programs to students only as a means for personal growth and exploration, never as a career option" (109). Some faculty in creative writing programs hold disdain for holistic approaches, believing they have been hired to aid in students' mastery of literary forms, and not to conduct group therapy. Wallace Stegner insists that

> . . . the worst writing classes with which I have had any experience have been the soft ones—the mutual-admiration societies in which whatever is said, if it is said well, is right. A teacher who permits that sort of atmosphere to develop gives his students a profoundly wrong impression of the profession and of the professional's obligations. (Stegner 33)

Authors of holistic pedagogy have cited writing workshops as being too destructively critical: In a book on writing groups, the authors make sure to define writing *groups* as distinct from writing *workshops*, advising that "those of you who have taken many writing workshops or been through an MFA program may be already burdened by 'instructional baggage.' You may need to distance yourself both from criticisms and from the kind of praise you've received in those settings to get back to what's in your heart." (Haines 37)

Iconic Pedagogy

> Unlike most of the other [literary interview collections] [The Paris Review] is concerned primarily with the craft of fiction. It tells us what fiction writers are as persons, where they get their material, how they work from day to day, and what they dream of writing.
> —Malcolm Cowley, Introduction, *Writers at Work:*
> *The Paris Review Interviews*, First Series (8)

> This is not an autobiography. It is, rather, a kind of curriculum
> vitae—my attempt to show how one writer was formed.
>   —Stephen King, *On Writing* (18)

Iconic pedagogy focuses on no one particular goal or outcome for the writer's education; instead its defining feature is its mode of delivery: the author. It is meant to encompass all those ideas and lessons about creative writing pedagogies promulgated by specific, usually famous, authors. Texts in this pedagogy can take the form of interviews, essays, (auto)biographies, memoirs, annotated editions of literary works, book shows, lectures, writer-in-residencies, documentaries— any portrayal of an author, first- or second-hand, that delivers ideas about creative writing or its pedagogy. Formative instances of iconic pedagogy—in which readers begin to see these various works and their authors in specific relation to *writers* and *the writing life*—might include the critical prefaces and notebooks of Henry James, the published diaries of writers such as Virginia Woolf and Anaïs Nin, and the Paris Review interview series, *Writers at Work*.

Within this type, a distinction can be made between *direct* and *indirect* iconic pedagogy. The former would consist of an author's explicit directives to aspiring writers, while the latter would involve the student writer learning by example. This directness or indirectness exists irrespective of whether the text is of primary or secondary authorship (i.e., an essay *about* an author could still include explicit educational mandates to students, while an essay *by* an author may still only teach by example). Historically, prior to the development of institutionalized creative writing studies, iconic pedagogy had been predominantly indirect and "by example," through literary biographies and interviews, or for a lucky few aspiring writers, through apprenticeships. But increasingly in modern times, it is carried out directly, and it becomes difficult to find texts by or about authors that do *not* address, implicitly or explicitly, the aspiring writer.

The particularity of each text of iconic pedagogy serves to circumscribe it within the larger realm of creative writing pedagogy; authors are tacitly conceptualized as practitioners in the field of writing pedagogy rather than its innovators and paradigm-shifters, adding their commentaries to an autonomous set of principles and dictates, while lesser-known authors of creative writing pedagogy texts function more as textbook writers or secondary researchers. So when Barbara Kingsolver says "As a professional storyteller, I take myths personally. I take it as part of my job to examine the stories that hold us together as a society and that we rely on to maintain our identity," (203) the statement may be contextualized by the reader's knowledge that Kingsolver is a socially conscious, activist, liberal feminist, as well as a commercially successful author. The student writers' acceptance of her indirect pedagogy may depend on their sympathy, or lack thereof, for these aspects of her public persona. The statement may then be subject to pedagogical preempting by more generalized, depoliticized, and decontextualized notions of what writing is, what writers do, and so on.

Iconic pedagogy speaks volumes about the overlap, and perhaps essential fusion, that now exists between literature/literary culture and writing/writerly culture. I don't mean this in the Barthesian sense of texts *lisible* and *scriptable*, but I would certainly invoke Foucault's idea of the *author-function* (1984), where ". . . an author's name is not simply an element in a discourse . . . it performs a certain role with regard to narrative discourse, assuming a classificatory function."(109) The reader can only make sense of literary texts when they have been organized and linked through an acquaintance with elements of the author as "writer"—lifestyle, habits, personality, publishing history, and so on—elements that are not essential or even intrinsically connected to the text in any demonstrable way, but are rather part of "the operations that we force texts to undergo, the connections that we make, the traits that we establish as pertinent, the continuities that we recognize, or the exclusions that we practice" (Foucault 110).

Conclusions

In so many ways, and perhaps to the ironic amusement of discourse theorists, it seems that the discourse of creative writing pedagogy has foregrounded itself at the expense of overtaking its own subject of study: *creative writing!* The valuation of self-reflexivity is of course an important development in postmodern thought, but when does self-reflexivity become narcissism? What kind of mirror is creative writing holding up to itself, and is it taking a good look at what's being reflected back? Are any of the mass market texts about creative writing truly, deeply, and critically self-reflexive? Do they point to paths of intellectual and creative exploration outside their own discourses, or do they set up hamster wheels of narcissistic "inspiration" and "guidance" for the aspiring writer? Which is an aspiring writer now more likely to turn to when in need of said guidance: a text of literary or topical interest, or a book or magazine that self-referentially speaks directly to "them" —the newest Natalie Goldberg, the latest *Poets and Writers*?

When it comes to academic creative writing programs, I see their decentralization and even dismantling as one of the most promising reforms that could be pursued. I don't mean this in a fatalistic sense, such that what's broken doesn't deserve fixing. In this I may follow R. V. Cassill, founder and first president of the Associated Writing Programs, who is reported by George Garrett to have made "a strong case for the deinstitutionalization of creative writing," characterizing the programs as "a good idea whose time had come and gone" (Garrett 59). But if degree-granting creative writing programs are to push on, undaunted by critics calling for their termination, how might they better contend with the deeply public and popular nature of creative writing practice? One way might be to have students earn part of their degree credits through a cultural practicum, and to include on a student's committee of advisors at least one member unaffiliated with academia, a link to a community in which the student writer has acknowledged an affinity or interest. This decentering of workshop hegemony would remind the writer that the MFA program is a fundamentally temporary and contingent community, and would extend Chris Green's idea about "putting the [creative writing] workshop in service to the student and the speech communities they represent" (161). For their part, those who study creative writing pedagogy need to begin looking beyond their frequent compare-and-contrasts with literary and composition/rhetoric pedagogies, to ask what pedagogical strategies have been employed in other areas of the fine arts—"a more thorough consideration of the artist in the university context," where "M.F.A. studio arts curricula have diverged so neatly from creative writing tenets" (Amato and Fleisher 12).

Ultimately, rather than repeating the constant anecdotes about how many pencils Hemingway sharpened before setting to work, the constant clichés and counter-clichés of writing what one does or doesn't know, and the constant romantic rhetoric of the writer as addict, outlaw, starving artist, or spiritual journeyer, students of creative writing need to begin to ask, and to attempt to answer, rigorously, over and over again, fundamental questions about the *ontologies* of all things written and writerly. Rather than the mantra of "what if . . .?" student writers need to ask "what is . . .?" What *is* language, what are its requisite properties, what are its malleable and shifty characteristics? What *is* writing—is it just the movement of the pencil across the paper, the impression of the typographic symbol; is it the act of creating grammatical formations, regardless of semantic content; is it the transcription of voices, the materialization of thoughts, the delivery of "messages"? And if it is any or all of these things, what does it mean to gather in a classroom with a group of strangers who have paid their tuition and filled out a timetable to try and practice and ostensibly improve upon it? What *is* an author—is it anyone who picks up a pen, is it a lifestyle, a gift and talent unavailable to mere "writers"? What is literature, how is it distinct from any other text or linguistic expression? What is a literary genre, why, who said so? Students cannot just stop at the tidy epigraphs—romantic, esoteric, mystical, or comforting—provided by their favourite authors *ad infinitum*. To ask these questions as a matter of course is to keep up a fight against stagnation, obsolescence, and irrelevance—not only in the student's personal life and creative work, but in language, literature, and culture at large.

In making these suggestions, I would rather err on the side of redundancy than to wait until every investigative stone has been upturned, though both are equally Sisyphean notions. Until we are further along in our explorations of creative writing pedagogy, I hope that my discussion and proposed typology will encourage all of us involved in creative writing to take a closer and more sustained look at popular pedagogies of creative writing, with all the ideas about writers and writing that they keep in circulation, inside the ivory tower and out.

Bibliography

Amato, Joe and H. Kassia Fletcher. 2003. "Reforming Creative Writing Pedagogy: History as Knowledge, Knowledge as Activism." *Electronic Book Review*, http://www.altx.com/ebr/riposte/rip2/rip2ped/amato.htm. Accessed April 16, 2003.

Braine, John. 1974. *Writing a Novel*. London: Eyre Methuen.

Burroway, Janet. 1987. *Writing Fiction: A Guide to Narrative Craft*. 2nd edition. Boston: Little, Brown and Company.

Diamant, Anita. 1991. "Between Writer and Agent." *The Writer's Handbook*. Sylvia K. Burack, ed. Boston, MA: The Writer Inc.

Epstein, Jason. 2002. *Book Business: publishing past, present, and future*. New York, NY: Norton.

Forster, E. M. 1962. *Aspects of the Novel*. Harmondsworth, Middlesex: Pelican.

Foucault, Michel. 1984. "What Is an Author?" In *The Foucault Reader*. Paul Rabinow, ed. New York: Pantheon, pp. 101–20.

Fuller, Robert C. 2001. *Spiritual, But Not Religious: Understanding Unchurched America*. New York, NY: Oxford University Press.

Garrett, George. 1989. "The Future of Creative Writing Programs." *Creative Writing in America: Theory and Pedagogy*. Joseph Moxley, ed. Urbana, IL: National Council of Teachers of English, pp. 47–61.

Goldberg, Natalie. 1986. *Writing Down the Bones*. Boston: Shambhala; [New York]: Random House.

Green, Chris. 2001. "Materializing the Sublime Reader: Cultural Studies, Reader Response, and Community Service in the Creative Writing Workshop." *College English*. 64.2 (November): 153–74.

Haines, Dawn Denham, Susan Newcomer, and Jacqueline Raphael. 1997. *Writing Together: How to Transform Your Writing in a Writing Group*. New York: Perigree.

Kingsolver, Barbara. 2002. "Household Words." *Small Wonder*. New York: Harper-Collins, pp. 195–205.

Lerner, Betsy. 2000. *The Forest for the Trees: An Editor's Advice to Writers*. New York: Riverhead Books.

North, Stephen. 1987. *The Making of Knowledge in Composition Studies: Portrait of an Emerging Field*. Upper Montclair, NJ: Boynton/Cook Publishers.

Rico, Gabriele. 1983. *Writing the Natural Way: Using Right-Brain Techniques to Release Your Expressive Powers*. Tarcher/Putnam.

Shelnutt, Eve. 1989. "Notes from a Cell: Creative Writing Programs in Isolation." In
    Creative Writing in America: Theory and Pedagogy. Joseph Moxley, ed. Urbana,
    IL: National Council of Teachers of English, pp. 3–24.

Starker, Stephen. 1989. *Oracle at the Supermarket: the American Preoccupation with
    Self-Help Books.* New Brunswick, NJ: Transaction.

Stegner, Wallace. 1988. *On the Teaching of Creative Writing.* Hanover, NH: University
    Press of New England.

Stevenson, John. 1983. *Writing Commercial Fiction.* Englewood Cliffs, NJ: Prentice-
    Hall.

8

Putting Wings on the Invisible

Voice, Authorship, and the Authentic Self

By Patrick Bizzaro and Michael McClanahan

What do student-writers expect to gain by studying writing in the academy? What, specifically, are their objectives, if they can voice them at all? How will their teachers help them reach their goals? Are the goals of young writers achievable? Can teachers teach the particular writing skills their students want to learn? Even if so, what are some of the problems posed when we begin to theorize what we do when we teach creative writing with the goal of helping students reach their often-idealized goals?

The following exchange between a recent MA in Creative Writing, Michael McClanahan, and one of his writing teachers, Patrick Bizzaro, explores issues that emerge when we ask the preceding questions, issues related to voice, authorship, and the authentic self in the postmodern age.

1

McClanahan: I'm a creative writing student because somewhere, somehow—like, through the influence of a high school English teacher—I discovered that words are special and that I have a special relationship with them. I'm in it for the art. But I've done other, less "artsy" writing in academia, business, and government. I've written for many reasons, but ultimately I write creatively because I "passed" Rilke's test and know that I "would have to die if it were denied" me to write. I write because, well, just because. I can't help myself. That, I suppose, is what makes me a writer in the same sense that a dog with fleas is a scratcher. Not that I'm the most elegant scratcher, or even one others would emulate. I just have to scratch. I'd love to make Stephen King-type money (and I *did* get paid for other types of writing), but I'll scratch for free if I have to.

On second thought, scratch the scratching analogy. It's rather crude. I prefer what Wallace Stevens said: "The poet is the priest of the invisible," even if that statement—if by analogy as well—begs certain questions and has become, in a sense, part of the ongoing folklore associated with creative writers who teach the "spiritual dimensions" of what they do when they write. To me, "priest of the invisible" is more like it. It's more mystical. More high and mighty. I'd rather think of myself as a proselyte priest than a dog with fleas. That's how I think of Stevens and that's how I think of you, Pat—as priests. After all, we're ultimately into stuff like self, voice, and identity. Invisible stuff like the stuff priests deal with. Maybe even into faith and godlike powers.

That's why it is imperative that I tell you what I want from you creative writing professors, from writing teachers of any writing course where serious, committed students can be found: I want you to show me the literary equivalent of the magic Michelangelo was talking about when he said the whole trick to art was to see "the angel in the marble," and carve until the angel is "free." I want you to show me how to *see*, and I want you to show me how to carve without cracking the halo. I want you to show me how to put wings on the invisible.

I could be asking too much, or maybe I'm just dense as good marble, because it's not getting through. Too often in writing classes today, I feel like Edward Rowland Sill who, according to D. G. Myers in *The Elephants Teach: Creative Writing Since 1880*, responded to his nineteenth-century professor's instructions to scan classical meter with the retort, "Please sir, I don't scan." Like Sill, I don't want to scan any more. I feel as though I'm beyond that. I can build a sentence, critique a poem, identify simile and scene and protagonist and antagonist and mood and setting and find all those traditional classroom answers. But they're getting old and so am I, so sometimes I get frustrated that you guys—you writing teachers—aren't interested in showing me what I really want to know, the tricks or magic or whatever you want to name it. It could be that you're not "priests" after all.

Maybe, though, Sill and I aren't unique in our frustration, if a couple of well-known phrases about writing and education are any indication. For one, Mark Twain said, "I never let schooling interfere with my education," and, for another, Charles Olson lamented that he was "uneducated" at Wesleyan, Yale, and Harvard. Those comments are rather scary to me because many of us proselyte priests are turning to the academy to find out how to break into the writing biz. Myers reports that in 1996, more than 300 creative writing programs were granting degrees in the United States, with a professional success rate for graduates of "about 1 percent (as compared with 90 percent for graduates of medical school)." Scary.

And speaking of Stephen King, he says in *On Writing: A Memoir of the Craft*, that he's "doubtful about writing classes, but not entirely against them." After all, he says, he met his future wife in a writing class so, in that case at least, the writing class could "hardly be counted as a total loss." Now, I don't want to get into the debate about whether King's writing demonstrates that he could have profited by paying less attention to Tabitha in writing class. I'd rather explore the dark reality that most creative writing students do not seem to "succeed" at any level as writers. I think failure might be a product of being unable to "see" or "imagine" or "perceive" the way great writers do.

But there is a bright side to this dark reality. Despite the ridiculously low success rate (whatever "success" means for a creative writer), Myers reports that about 85 percent of the 135 poets chosen to appear in *The Best American Poetry* for 1990 and 1991 were graduates, professors, or administrators of creative writing programs (sometimes all three). But there's another "but" here (you know that "but" is the most dangerous word in the English language, don't you?). And the "but" is that the 85 percent statistic might not mean that writing programs are working, but that writing teachers who "succeed" might select work for recognition when it sounds like their own. With this in mind, it may be very difficult, and perhaps even professionally suicidal, for a writing student to consciously avoid sounding like the teacher.

But if you writers-who-teach, to borrow Wendy Bishop's term for them, are priests, you'd never stoop to that kind of thing, would you? You wouldn't require that we work in a narrow range of possibilities in poetry, fiction, non-fiction, and drama, would you? That would be like excommunicating a young Galileo, wouldn't it? You don't want the sun to revolve around the earth forever, do you?

You just can't, because you're "it" for American creative writing students. The *teaching* you do, as much if not more than the *writing* you do, is very important. Since Sill became one of the first to combine his writing with the teaching of writing many others have done the same, and now we proselyte priests look for programs that feature instruction from successful writers whose work we admire. I have not found a program where Stephen King teaches (maybe the fact that his writing has made him a zillionaire is relevant), but despite his "uneducation" Olson became a teacher.

So I'm curious. Why did Olson become a teacher while King did not? As far as I know, Olson never got rich from his writing, so it makes me wonder if all writers who become teachers do so just to make ends meet. But King wrote a book about the craft of writing when he didn't need the money such a book might generate. So I also wonder if there's not something in writers that compels them to somehow share the innermost secrets of what makes them what they are.

I hope there is such a force in writers, because if I'm willing to write for free, I want you to be willing to teach when you become a zillionaire. Otherwise you're teaching what you no longer believe in yourself. What kind of priest is that? It's impossible to ignore the fact that throughout my creative writing education, professors constantly remind me of the "real world," and that because of it I should build credentials to become competitive for teaching jobs.

But I want to be a writer. A good writer. A great writer. And since "85 percent of the 135 poets chosen to appear in *The Best American Poetry* for 1990 and 1991 were graduates, professors, or administrators of creative writing programs," I'm convinced that I need your help to do it. How will you help me? Scansion? I don't think that's the approach Olson took or even one you'd like to adopt. Just look at the Black Mountain College experiment. And look at Allen Ginsberg and the Jack Kerouac School of Disembodied Poetics he established with Anne Waldman at Naropa University in 1974. In fact, let's look a little closer at Olson and Ginsberg. As postmodernists, they might have something new to offer.

Let's start with their mutual search for what lies within the artist. Their awareness of their internal energy, combined with a rejection of western habits of logic and classification (scansion?) essentially define postmodernism, particularly to Olson. As Olson wrote in his manifesto, "Projective Verse," "A poem is energy transferred from where the poet got it . . . by way of the poem itself to, all the way over to, the reader . . . the poem itself must, at all points, be a high energy-construct and, at all points, an energy-discharge."

Yeah. Preach it, Brother Olson. That's the kind of thing I'm looking for. That's finding an angel in the marble.

Now it's your turn, Pat. Preach. What is a poem to you? Should writers deliberate upon their own definitions? What is poetry right now? What do you think it will become? And preach about the "real world" stuff I've already mentioned. What have other writers, historically, seen as the role of writing in their lives? And speaking of seeing, do writers see differently from other artists?

What about "schooling?" What role do you believe "schooling" has in the development of writing skills, historically? Does a student ever really become a teacher? Does a teacher ever stop being a student? What is the impact on teaching and writing when you mix the two?

Ultimately, what goals are reasonable for creative writing students? Is there a mold we should fit into, or a mold we should strive to break? What is "success" for a creative writer, anyway? Is it a good thing that academe has such an influence on creative writing?

2

Bizzaro: These are very demanding questions, Mike. I'll do my best with them, of course, but I also want to caution you that these are questions you should think through, too, especially as you prepare to teach the various writing courses we all end up teaching.

Let's start, then, at the beginning: Why do writers write? I think most people of my generation who became writers did so because writing to them was a way of not only expressing, but of discovering the *self* . . . and my generation's student-writers are now your writer-teachers. One of my favorite poets, Galway Kinnell, says that "poetry is deeper than personality." That view of writing is critical to me, because Kinnell speaks from a perspective on writing that was popular in the sixties and seventies, not just for creative writers like us, but for writers in general, including those who took composition courses. And this view has influenced and continues to influence the way many students have been taught how to write, especially in creative writing courses. In this view of writing and the writer, writing is seen as an expression of the self. It was popular in those days for teachers (of composition as well as creative writing) to insist that the highest endeavor for a writing student like you or me was to discover his or her *voice*.

As you might surmise from my hesitance in using terms like self and voice, these terms and the view of writing they suggest have become very problematic over the past fifteen years. The view that voice is associated with self is a neo-Romantic notion, one that draws a picture of a writer working in isolation in an effort to express an authentic self, a self that 150 years later Kinnell would say is deeper than personality. So certain were writing teachers of the late sixties and early seventies that a self exists and that a writer simply needs to be given an opportunity to find it that one important teacher/theorist, Peter Elbow, claimed to have taught himself how to write doctoral-level texts (his dissertation) and then wrote in a more formal way *Writing Without Teachers*, a book about how that phenomenal experience might take place for other people. The premise of Elbow's book is that writing is a natural, even an organic, process. Elbow uses the metaphors of *growing* and *cooking*, for instance, to describe the *natural* process of writing.

But this Romantic (what some call *expressivist* or *expressionist*) approach to writing instruction was soon challenged in composition studies by those who saw writing as a *cognitive activity*—that is, as a process of intellection students could learn how to do by imitating the behaviors of good or experienced writers—and soon thereafter who saw writing and students themselves as products of the culture in which they live. Those who argue for the influence of culture on the development of individual identity—*social constructionists* or *social epistemics*—argue that there is no such thing as an autonomous self. As a result, teaching that was intended to produce voice was off target, wrong in its assumptions about writers, who they are and what they do. So the social constructionists, led by James Berlin, were the most outspoken adversaries of the neo-Romantic attitude toward writing. They were advocates, instead, of the notion that all selves are socially constructed, not autonomous at all. Creative writers and teachers of creative writing did not know (and many still do not know) that they were the ones being spoken to and about. Most creative writers I know reject the notion forwarded by social constructionists, that writing is *not* the expression of an autonomous self. Most continue to believe when they teach their students to write that writers write to discover or express this self.

It's important to me to say that the view that denies the existence of self and voice often makes me uncomfortable, too. But my concern has more to do with the fact other writers—creative writing purists, I like to call them—attribute their discomfort to the ascendancy of theory in the academy. I have come to call it the compositioning of creative writing. After all, one theorist calls into question whether authorship can be said to actually exist (Foucault describes authorship in various ways, including as "a voluntary obliteration of the self," which oddly echoes T. S. Eliot's sense that poetry is "an extinction of self"). If we are all simply constructions, then the author is more an impersonal *principle*, as Foucault would have it, than an actual person. Rather than seeking life and even immortality, accordingly, authorship is associated with death (obliteration) for Foucault. The author as principle simply records the occurrences of culture; it is inevitable that an author will function in this role. Foucault writes, "We can easily imagine a culture where discourse would circulate without any need for an author" (148). You might come to agree with the logic that led Foucault to this view. But as a writer, I cannot imagine you would live comfortably with this view, at least not for long. I think you and I and most other seriously committed writers think of writing as an actualization of the self and then, in the sound of our words, we'd like to believe we hear our autonomous voices. I'm not sure if what I have to say here pleases you, Mike.

But you and I and most serious writers want to believe there is some reason for writing beyond simply expressing the culture we live in (or just getting a required course out of the way). Perhaps limiting our reasons for writing in any way is too sweeping because I do believe we express that culture. But I also want to believe there's something more. And your questions bring it to mind for me because for me a large part of what I do as a writer is show people how I see things, how I *perceive*. Historically, of course, vision and perception and seeing have had powerful advocates among our strongest writers.

As a reader and student of literary study, I've always been interested in the way writers *see* since I think once a student writes something—I mean, really writes something new—the student will be changed forever not only by what is written but also by the process of seeing it, of getting it written. I believe the reason writing changes the writer has quite a bit to do with what the writer has come to see. One very seductive aspect of *voice* is that it expresses a personal articulation of what we understand to be true about the world.

One of my favorite authors, William Blake, says in "The Marriage of Heaven and Hell," "If the doors of perception were cleansed every thing would appear to man as it is, infinite" (107). I like the notion of cleansing those doors, risky though it has been for some writers to do so, and I think Blake means by *perception* what you mean when you use the word *see* as you do. There are lots of ways of perceiving, of seeing. Maybe we can define them in some systematic way, but maybe not. This is a very complex issue historically, and it is a very complex issue for young writers: Where do they look to find a viable subject, and how should they look at it?

Blake may not be a great role model here, though he certainly is interesting to think about. But perception to Blake was more like hallucination or vision (these are ways of seeing too, aren't they?). Still, from his perspective, if we don't cleanse those doors, we'll see "all things thro' narrow chinks of [our] cavern" (107), and I guess that would be bad or a failure of some kind— I think, for Blake, the result would be bad poetry, lack or loss of vision. Blake is one of those prototype Romantics who has influenced the way we continue to talk about seeing as artists and writers. After all, neo-Romantic thinking about writing comes from efforts to imagine intensely and theorize such efforts (the Romantics spent a lot of time theorizing the writing of poetry— something we're afraid to do much of these days). Wordsworth writes in Book Fourteen of *The Prelude,* "the mind of man becomes/ a thousand times more beautiful than the earth/ on which he dwells" (423). One of your favorite poets, Allen Ginsberg, took the notion of perception, as Blake advocates it, to new levels of experimentation, often using drugs as a kind of muse (though we all remember the story of Coleridge writing "Kubla Khan," which makes me believe Ginsberg was never alone in these actions). I don't recommend that my students go to such extremes, and that's not only because I think they've already spent enough money on books and supplies! My students often ask, nonetheless, if I think they should write under the influence of alcohol or drugs. My advice on this is consistent: never waste an experience. Less exotic than my advice but more influential, Elbow must have been greatly impressed by some of the ideas Wordsworth espoused, if not entirely by Wordsworth's texts themselves (Elbow claims to have not read much of Wordsworth's works and, specifically, not Wordsworth's "Preface").

Coleridge was another who influenced the way we talk about the way a writer sees, calling his way of seeing *imagination* rather than *perception* (and some would argue for a subtle difference between the two). Among other things, Coleridge differentiated the primary from the secondary imagination in Chapter Thirteen of *Biographia Literaria.* What most interests me as a writer is Coleridge's notion that primary imagination is "the living Power and prime Agent of all human Perception" (567), what some might call God. For Coleridge, the primary imagination, then, acts in creation of the sort and magnitude ("degree") we can only attribute to God (though belief in God was a source of conflict for Coleridge). Let me stress that no matter how egotistical writers seem to be, what they have as writers is *not* the primary imagination at all, but the secondary, what Coleridge defines as "an echo of the former." The secondary imagination is the godlike capacity in humans to "recreate." Coleridge says secondary imagination is "identical with the primary in the *kind* of its agency, and differing only in *degree*, and in the *mode* of its operation." I think of this definition of secondary imagination whenever I think of a novelist or short story writer making a world different (but consistently so) in its operation from the world in which we live—and this kind of authorship would, indeed, challenge Foucault's theory. This authorship is *godlike* in its capacity, if not altogether in the range of God's prime movement. And it takes courage as well as skill to see as though through the eyes of a god! In his *A Defence of Poetry*, Shelley argues that poets are the moral, if unacknowledged, legislators of the world. He thinks that way because he believes poets differ from other people specifically in what and how they see. (Wordsworth calls this "sensibility" in his "Preface" to *Lyrical Ballads*.) This discussion of Romantic writers is circular, of course, because most people would say we no longer live in a Romantic age. I would argue that creative writing instruction has at least part of its theoretical basis in Romanticism and Expressivism. Creative writing instruction may still, then, be in *its* Romantic age.

But most young writers will be more comfortable writing from logic and reason than from some sort of transcendent vision in an effort to recreate the operations of a world we recognize as similar in most ways to the one in which we live. Alexander Pope says in *An Essay on Man*, "Whatever is, Is right!" I'm not sure I agree with that view of things, but it is a viable view, one most people will feel comfortable with these days. But I'm also thinking of Slam Poetry, subjects and many times language itself taken right off the pages of newspapers. Often what I've heard of Slam Poetry is in the language of outrage and discontent. While much of it is Promethean, little of it has vision of the sort Blake and Coleridge and Shelley advocate. This all seems academic to me, and you rightly express your concern about formal schooling.

After all, there are mixed views about "academic creative writing," and I have them too. There are those, of course, who believe writers are born to write, that they possess the "writer gene." There have long been clubs and literary movements that provided a kind of "schooling," albeit informal. And some wannabe writers would follow powerful personalities, such as Coleridge, whose writing they wanted to imitate. But until recently, no one has actually attempted to trace the history of creative writing instruction. The first scholar to attempt such a study, D. G. Myers (in *The Elephants Teach*), traces creative writing programs in the United States since 1880 only. Most of those who have written histories of instruction in composition only go back about that far themselves. Prior to that writers often taught themselves how to write by composing in the manner, style, and often on the subjects of successful writers—employing modeling. I'm certain people learn how to do something in this fashion, having learned how to generate various kinds of texts myself in exactly this way. But is that *writing*? In a first-year composition class, for instance, we employ this kind of teaching when we ask students to read an essay and then reproduce something like it. As a creative writer, though, you can imagine how frustrating it might be to read Wallace Stevens' "Sunday Morning" and then try to write such a beast. Of course, this is not the same as reading Bruce Catton's essay on Lee and Grant and then writing a comparison/contrast essay on any subject of your choosing. Or reading a validation report written by someone on the job and then writing one for yourself.

But the modeling predicament doesn't stop there. I'm concerned to a certain extent to hear you say you think some students are rewarded for writing poems and stories and essays that sound like their teachers' work. As you know, a few years ago (in 1993, to be exact), I wrote a book entitled *Responding to Student Poems: Applications of Critical Theory*. My concern at the time was that teachers have historically appropriated their students' writings. Though I wrote that book about poetry, I could have included student essays among those texts teachers typically appropriate. I decided to write about poems, though, because so little thought had been given up until then about how we should comment on our students' work. The sense of it was that students are apprentices studying with masters, and the masters could help students revise their poems into respectability. Having felt irresponsible and phony at times dominating my students through comments and changes *I'd* make to *their* poems, I wondered if I could use theories for reading literary texts heretofore employed only with "sanctioned" literature in responding to my students' poems. The result wasn't a simple waste of time. I gave serious thought to ways of returning authority for a poem or story to the author, even if the author is a student.

That book was long out of print when I decided we have done too little examination of the causes for our dominance of students in creative writing and began some archival research. I found a very interesting book, *Teaching Creative Writing*, published in 1937 as "A Publication of the Progressive Education Association." The author, Lawrence H. Conrad, writes about the then-current view of creative writing students: "With our increased knowledge of the needs and aptitudes of the adolescent years, we have come to set a higher value upon creative practices wherever they may be introduced in the curriculum . . . ." (209). We have lost sight of influences on the way we teach creative writing and how they have lingered in our pedagogies. One of those influences, the one that endorses a creative writing teacher's appropriation of student texts, thus can be attributed to Progressive Education. Conrad continues by describing creative writing as a record of the emotional and psychological development of students: "teachers were urged to recognize the *unconscious* as the real source of motivation and behavior in themselves and their students. The essential task of education was seen as one of *sublimating* the child's *repressed* emotion into socially useful channels" (emphasis added, 209). This view of the purpose for having students write creatively is consistent, according to Myers, with the view espoused by Dewey that "any education that seeks the goal of training students for useful ends, as determined by people other than the students . . . is a form of ideological conditioning, preparing the many for lives as mere functionaries." What's more, the Freudian implications for teaching creative writing are clear.

I wasn't surprised, then, to read a few moments later the advice Conrad offered teachers in how they should respond to their students' creative writing:

> The teacher of such a [creative writing] course will be in a good position to guide students who are in difficulty, and to recommend guidance to those who require the attention of someone specially trained in psychiatry or in medicine . . . . If the vital bond of confidence is not to be broken, however, such a recommendation would normally be made to the student rather than to the school authorities, and the teacher's full influence should be exerted toward having the student take the first step toward treatment. (8)

Creative writing was seen as an opportunity for teachers to create "good citizens," a non-surprising outcome of the post-WW I era. Educators, then, viewed language as the representation of a student's inner self. And if, in the judgment of the teacher, that inner self failed to reveal conformity, the student would be advised to seek counseling.

I'm interested in ways that this attitude toward creative writing has stayed in some of our pedagogical choices, including how we respond to student writing and why we respond that way. One of the great strengths and great drawbacks of the kind of teaching usually associated with creative writing programs (and in recent years used in classes in composition, technical and business writing, and even scientific writing) is a product of what we call the *workshop method* of instruction. The underlying belief in teaching this way, a belief consistent with the continuing demand that practitioners (that is, those who produce that kind of writing) teach what they do, is that the best teachers of a particular type or genre of writing are writers skilled in producing that kind of writing. That view has resulted in the hiring of published poets, novelists, screenwriters, and creative essayists to teach creative writing. This is a wonderful thing: the opportunity for students to talk with writers actively engaged in finding solutions to the same kinds of problems in writing the students must solve for themselves. But there is a down side: this kind of teaching fosters master-apprentice relationships, the teacher having near dictatorial control over the students' texts. The logic is pretty simple. If students don't make the kinds of changes their teachers, who have appropriated their texts, recommend, they will receive poor grades. I heard one teacher, a well-known writer, say that her students could decide to not make the revisions she suggested; students, she argued, have a right to fail. Sometimes this kind of enforcement is more subtle, but it's usually there unless teachers do something consciously to prevent it from showing up. In any event, in my opinion, such teaching has produced a generation of clones—students who sound amazingly like their teachers. And because their teachers have some influence over what gets published and wins awards, this sameness is perpetuated in the magazines and journals that publish creative writing. Some writers have noted the limitations of the workshop method of instruction. But it continues, not because well-thought-out research studies have proved its effectiveness, but because tradition and privilege are such powerful forces that this long-standing method of instruction rarely is challenged. At the least, though, I think teachers overseeing workshops should learn how to comment on their students' writing without appropriating what's been written.

This discussion brings to mind for me an article in a recent issue of *College English*. In it, Kelly Ritter notes the large number (over 40 at last count) of Ph.D. creative writing programs that in recent years have come to compete with MFA programs. There's no easy dichotomy to be made here, but Ritter suggests that the Ph.D. has become more of a teaching degree and the MFA a writing degree. Not that Ph.D. graduates in creative writing don't write or that MFA graduates don't teach. It's just that many of them do much more in an English department than write and teach creative writing. They often specialize in writing and combine their interest in creative writing with an interest in all the other kinds of writing that go on in the university. Do writers long to become great teachers? Probably some do, probably an increasing number since the advent of the Ph.D. in creative writing and the increased need for teachers to teach the large numbers of students who want to take creative writing courses.

Success for writers can be a great many things. I like to talk to my students about Robert Browning, whose writing style changed dramatically during his lifetime, from writing poems of the sort popularized (by Shelley, in particular) during the time he lived to writing dramatic monologues. I can imagine a friend or relative of Browning looking at these strange writings ("Andrea del Sarto," "My Last Duchess," etc.) and wondering what on earth ole Bobby was thinking. In fact, he didn't have much of a readership during his lifetime and some people believe it's because the poems he wrote did not fit comfortably into anything they had ever seen before. I think it must be very difficult for a thoroughly new mode of writing to find its audience. I laugh, for instance, when I think of the difficulty T. S. Eliot would have trying to publish "The Waste Land" these days, so different is that poem from what we regularly see in our literary journals. I think an editor wants to see something at least in some small way familiar. So success, then, might not necessarily come from offering an editor something innovative, despite Ezra Pounds' urging to "make it new!"

I think writers quite naturally set goals, but I also think that sometimes the goals they set are unreasonable. To use a cliché, we must take our successes where we find them. I know my poetry has evolved over the past twenty years as my expectations for my poetry and my understanding of poetry have changed. Maybe I've become overly occupied with becoming a better teacher of creative writing. Some of my colleagues might think my emphasis is in the wrong place. My friend, Joe David Bellamy, has written an article in which he defends the writing program at Iowa (which has produced, in addition to Joe, dozens, maybe hundreds, of famous writers) but also argues that writers belong in the university: "Like it or not, there really is no place else for writers to go other than the university in American culture" (109). This means, of course, they will be teachers. I'd like to think Joe and I agree that there's another space in which writers can work comfortably at becoming better writers *and* better teachers of writing. So, yes, the notion of success is quite arbitrary. I want to think a writer who has become a great teacher of writing has succeeded much as the well-published author has succeeded.

Still, I know some writers who absolutely hate teaching. They think they spend too much time doing it and that the university should provide them with the time they want to write. I wouldn't mind that myself. But I object to the notion that working with students somehow hurts a teacher's writing. I've enjoyed the teaching I do, all of it—from composition to technical writing to my graduate poetry writing workshops—because I enjoy the community of writers I find myself in. I have to admit that my experiences teaching first-year composition have less frequently led me to a community of writers than, say, my graduate workshops. But even in comp I have felt myself as part of a group of writers, the oldest member of course! And the feeling of belonging is a powerful reward for me.

From at least one time-honored perspective, teaching writing is consistent with the goals of writing itself: that we instruct and delight through our writing. If more teachers took seriously the dictum that teaching involves delighting as well as informing, their classes wouldn't be nearly as deadly as they most often are. But as a critic, I still think of myself as someone who needs to learn more, and I write critical articles and book reviews with the goal of learning what I can from my peers. By reading contemporary works *as* a writer, I keep track of trends and note new ways writers solve old problems. But can I predict where poetry is going? Only a fool would offer such an opinion, so let me give it a try.

But let me generalize more about all sorts of writing rather than just about poetry. I'm not kidding when I tell you that back in the early seventies, when I took my first full-time teaching job at Northern Virginia Community College, people were talking and writing about how computers would eventually do our writing for us. I was nervous, as a teacher teaching composition, business writing, journalism, and creative writing, that computers would replace me entirely. Of course, that never happened—at least not entirely. As far as I know (unless something new has happened), computers cannot make human decisions, adapt to different audiences, express feeling. At least not yet. Or, more specifically, the computer I'm pounding on right now cannot do those things. If it could, our entire notion about what writing is would have to change.

What I have noticed is that writing has become much more functional. People who thought their computers would write for them have ended up taking seminars on the job in order to learn how to improve their writing skills. (I'm surprised to note nowadays how many people who are trained as poets or, at least, who write poetry, also do this double duty in teaching writing semi-nars in business and industry.) This is what's happening: These days, no one is exempt from having to write. The construction guys who just remodeled our bathrooms do more writing than you might suspect. Teachers write all kinds of observations and reflections and evaluations. These are all worthwhile kinds of writings. They're not always poems or stories, but they still come from see-ing and attempting to be heard.

As a creative writer myself—and you and I have discussed this before—I sometimes worry that I spend too much time doing "non-creative writing." This writing includes grant proposals, articles on teaching composition, textbooks, literary criticism, my part of *this*—whatever it is or will become! But it also includes syllabi, course packets, comments on student writing—job-related stuff. The point is that many who thought they would spend all their days writing poems and stories also find out they must do this other, mundane writing. I'm in that group. So any definition I would give to writing would need to express my belief that people have to learn how to write a variety of kinds of texts and adapt them to different audiences and purposes. I also want to insist on the necessity that we use writing in the civic arena to understand the terms of our lifestyles and to express our views concerning when those lifestyles must change.

3

McClanahan: There it is! The magic word! *Lifestyle.* Everything you've told me seems to boil down to this. Writing is a way of life, a style of being often defined more by the questions we ask than by the answers we provide. Writ-ers live on a journey to unknown places. That would explain the debate about what writers are and what we do—the *fuzziness* of it all. A writer's life is a question that breeds questions. That helps me see why it is so tough to be both a writer and a teacher. Teachers are supposed to provide answers, but how can a writer, who lives to ask, do that?

I have demanded much from you. I've sought answers, and you've responded with context. Rightly so, because I see that answers are dangerous things. They can stop the itch. If that happens, I might stop scratching.

4

Bizzaro: But really, Mike. I hope I haven't pretended to know much of any-thing. I'm certainly a good one to ask if you are willing to let someone move around in language and actually make an effort to not provide a definite answer.

Let me end by saying I'd like to think I have some knowledge about the history of writing, which has led me to the formulation of many, many diffi-cult questions I probably will never really be able to answer. One thing I know for certain is that I've enjoyed being a teacher, no matter what else I might be—writer, father, football coach. And I can truly say I have enjoyed working with you in my classes, Mike, and on this little essay, if that's what it is. Your questions are good ones; you've challenged me at every turn and that will make me a better teacher.

Bibliography

Bellamy, Joe David. 1995."The Iowa Mystique and Those Who Loathe It." *Literary Luxuries: American Writing at the End of the Millennium*. Columbia, Missouri: University of Missouri Press.

Bizzaro, Patrick. 1993. *Responding to Student Poems: Applications of Critical Theory*. Urbana, Illinois: National Council of Teachers of English.

—— and Resa Crane Bizzaro. 1999. Unpublished Interview with Peter Elbow.

Blake, William. 1995. "The Marriage of Heaven and Hell." *English Romantic Writers,* 2nd edition. David Perkins, ed. NY: Harcourt Brace.

Coleridge, Samuel Taylor, 1995. *Biographia Literaria. English Romantic Writers,* 2nd edition. David Perkins, ed. NY: Harcourt Brace.

Conrad, Lawrence H. 1937. *Teaching Creative Writing*. NY Appleton.

Elbow, Peter. 1973. *Writing Without Teachers*. NY: Oxford University Press.

Foucault, Michel. 1990. "What Is An Author?" *Critical Theory Since 1965*. Hazard Adams and Leroy Searle, eds. Tallahassee, FL: Florida State University Press.

King, Stephen. 2000. *On Writing: A Memoir of the Craft*. NY: Scribner's.

Myers, D. G. 1996. *The Elephants Teach: Creative Writing Since 1880*. Englewood Cliffs, NJ: Prentice Hall.

Ritter, Kelly. 2001. "Professional Writers/Writing Professionals: Revamping Teacher Training in Creative Writing Ph.D. Programs." *College English* 64.2: 205–27.

9

Box Office Poison

The Influence of Writers in Films on Writers (in Graduate Programs)

By Wendy Bishop and Stephen Armstrong

It's a tossup as to which film type is more boring—movies about writers or movies about drunks and drug addicts. The former films try to dramatize what it's like to be creative on paper, while the latter try to analyze the self-destruction of losers.
—Joe Baltake, *Sacramento Bee*
movie critic, on *Big Bad Love*

When I picture writing, I often see a solitary writer alone in a cold garret working into the small hours of the morning by the thin light of a candle. It seems a curious image to conjure, for I am absent from this scene in which the writer is an Author and the writing is Literature. In fact it is not my scene at all.
—Linda Brodkey (49).

We both write, teach writing, and gravitate toward films about writers, fully aware that critics often disdain them, general audiences tend to ignore them, and producers consider them to be box office poison. Nevertheless, some of these films have been hits—like *Misery*, *Almost Famous,* and *Finding Forrester*—while others have become cult favorites, especially with academics—*His Girl Friday*, *Citizen Kane*, *Barton Fink*, and *Henry Fool*. The popularity and pervasiveness of these films and their portrayals of the writing life, including life in college writing programs (consider *Wonder Boys*, *Storytelling*, and *Orange County)* suggest that it's worth considering how someone new to the writing profession, as well as the writing instruction profession, picks up pointers by viewing these images of writers. We feel it would be beneficial for writers and instructors to consider these influences when entering a graduate program and participating in or conducting a writing workshop, and to cast these images anew in the service of better representing writers to the general public, to writing students, to ourselves as writers on a lifetime journey in letters.

Like most individuals in the United States, we search for public images and stories that reflect our own experiences and profession. We know that writers in films often receive a heroic or a romantic treatment as the film industry, for several decades, has compensated for the "problem" of depicting cognition and text-production by (re)creating writers as tough guys, war correspondents, investigative reporters, beautiful losers, and male WASP (think Hemingway) geniuses. Given this sort of influence, these movies are box office poison in a new sense because we derive from them—tacitly or explicitly— models of behavior or turn to them as mirrors for understanding. This suggests that movies about writers can overinfluence the classroom and writing community with their problematic and often inauthentic depictions of the writers' lifestyle options and composing processes.

In the course of analyzing the depiction of writers in film, we have compiled a list of movies that showcase writers or comment on the writing process and we use these to provide an analysis and typology of writer types, writers' roles, and writing practices (see Appendix A). In this chapter, we offer a first report of what is proving to be an instructive and longer-term project. We look, in particular, at how these images may be informing the graduate curriculum. After considering the most commonly circulated of these "received" images, we suggest some of the pedagogical problems they can foster and offer ideas for using these images more productively. By asking what it means to teach— or "unteach"—these images, we aim to reconstruct a better, more useful account of the writing life.

Writer as Film and Cultural Icon

Everyone's a film critic, particularly when it comes to movies depicting writers, and it does not take long to find a preponderance of negative opinions about such films. After watching *Orange County* and reading some on-line reviews of this sort of film, we searched the Internet and found a number of reviews like that of Joe Baltake, the *Sacramento Bee* movie critic whose quote opens this chapter. Like so many others, he suggests enough is enough, that no one should make movies about writers because they're boring and self-serving. Nevertheless, after having enjoyed movies such as *Misery* and *Adaptation*, after encountering a writing student's claim that *Wonder Boys* was the key element in propelling him to enroll in a writing course, and after discussions with our peers, swapping names of films that centered on the writing life that we found compelling, our interest in and appreciation for this film genre increased. We then more systematically contacted friends and colleagues for film titles and searched through collections at video stores and libraries. Next, we journaled collaboratively for several weeks, developing our thoughts, discussing our frustrations with the depictions of writers as we found them (and confirming our continued fascination with these images), wondering all the while about the influence of the depictions on writers and writing teachers in the classroom.

Eventually, we constructed an alphabetical list of well-known movies in which writer-characters appear, and from this, we were able to identify commonly recurring types and characteristics. For instance, we found that most male writers in film honor the expected stereotype of the "macho hero," while most females honor the stereotype of "cute nuisance" or "sheep in wolf's clothing" (hence, a "macho woman"); and minorities and homosexuals are rarely portrayed. Then, as we developed a typological list, grouping depictions by the traits the writers in each category share in common (and dividing depictions by the way they differ), we generated lists of films in which the types are present:

- The Action Hero: *Blood on the Sun, Julia, Foreign Correspondent, The Battle of Anzio, True Crime*
- The Disoriented Woman: *Absence of Malice, Lifeboat, The Legend of Lylah Clare, Romancing the Stone, Iris*
- The Mad MAN: *Sweet Smell of Success, The Shining, Big Bad Love, Beyond a Reasonable Doubt, The Lost Weekend, Laura*
- The Master Writer: *Misery, Wilde, Kafka, F for Fake, As Good as it Gets*
- The Male Ingenue: *Almost Famous, Finding Forrester, The Basketball Diaries*
- The Reporter: *Citizen Kane, The Front Page, Absence of Malice, His Girl Friday, Lifeboat, Meet John Doe*
- The Screenwriter and The Playwright: *Sunset Boulevard, All About Eve, Sudden Fear, Adaptation, Barton Fink*
- The Writer Who Doesn't Write: *Under the Volcano, Royal Tannenbaums, All the King's Men, The Third Man*
- The Writing Program: *Wonder Boys, Storytelling, Orange County*

The typical "writer," we discovered, offers a film version of compositionist Linda Brodkey's "solitary writer" in that he is male. "In much of literary modernism," she explains, "solitude is at once inevitable and consequential, the irremediable human condition from which there is no escape. And whenever writers are pictured there, as they so often are, the writer-writers-alone is a narrative of irreconcilable alienation, a vicarious narrative told by an outsider who observes rather than witnesses life" (398). The typical film writer differs from Brodkey's modernist literary writer, however, in that he dominates his films. We rarely see him writing, but we often see him as a successful *character*, brawling, drinking, a creative and self-destructive genius, a lone wolf with an active social life.

Meanwhile, the physical act of writing by persons labeled as writers rarely appears on the screen. Instead, these characters tend to spend the bulk of their time conducting research for their work (*Citizen Kane, Beyond a Reasonable Doubt, Foreign Correspondent*); or experiencing (frequently) the negative consequences that result from their work's publication (*The Ring*). Most often, writers are presented as professionals, usually affiliated with newspapers (*Call Northside777, Blood on the Sun*). And more often than not, this cinematic "show-don't-tell" requirement entails putting the characters into situations that cannot occur at or near the place where writers actually work, like the desk or table. In order to keep the writer character true to its type, the filmmaker must displace the act of writing and substitute those stages of the writing process in which there is more likely to be action.

Usually this means that the filmmaker emphasizes the time and activities that occur before the act of writing. A supreme example of this is *Citizen Kane*, in which a reporter sets out to discover the meaning of the publishing magnate's cryptic last word, "Rosebud." Less often, filmmakers also focus on the consequences of the writing act. A good example of this is *Absence of Malice*, a film in which a reporter attempts to correct the problems she's created for an innocent man by writing a slanderous article. Ivor Montagu—an esteemed filmmaker and critic who assisted both Eisenstein and Hitchcock—explains why this shift from act to action is necessary.

> "Moving picture" or "motion picture"–the significance of this term is that it implies that the object (process or experience) described has two aspects, both equally essential. It is a *picture*, that is, it is a representation, not actual, not real, and it conveys *the appearance of motion*. (13)

The depiction of the writer on film, engaged in the act of writing, therefore, is inherently nondramatic. As link between the metaphysical and the real, all we would see, were this depicted on the screen, would be a person sitting hunched over a desk, moving his or her hands. Thus films with writers in them keep the depiction of *the act of writing* to a minimum. If, in a movie, a writer has writer's block—a conflict but often a highly inactive one—the filmmaker will not be able to portray the struggle in a manner that is both dramatic and realistic because the true location of the conflict is within in the mind, and the hands can only move after the conflict, at least temporarily, has been resolved. Moreover, filmmakers cannot present writers writing in the ways they most often write—that is, alone, placing words on paper or computer screen. Instead, they must put their characters into situations in which action and movement occur visually, vividly, constantly. In other words, the writer-writes-alone resists representation in film. Instead, audiences (and students of writing who watch films about writers) view the writer in actions-other-than-writing—frequently presented in a social setting, where the writer interacts (chats, fights, interviews) with other people. This nonwriting behavior, however, appeals to audiences romantically, as well, by presenting the writing life as an adventurous one, a life audiences (and students of writing) may connect with vicariously.

Again, according to Ivor Montagu, the most successful films—the ones that encourage viewers to associate themselves with the story's characters to the highest degree—are those in which the filmmakers rely on pictorial rendering, a strategy that avoids the use of nonvisual elements such as music, dialogue, commentary (114). A film must present its conflicts, characterizations, and narrative in a manner that keeps the use of words—through speech, intertitles, hand-written letters, and so forth—to a minimum. Depicting the act of writing therefore obliges the filmmaker to construct scenarios that are often dramatically and visually satisfying at the cost of verity. Because the act of writing itself requires little movement from the human figure—in contrast, say, to avoiding gunfire in an open field—it is visually uninteresting on the movie screen. To compensate for this lack of action, the filmmaker must resort to "noncinematic" efforts—such as a voiceover reading of the text as it is being written—or "nonrealistic" tricks—such as a symbolic and thus imprecise and abstract representation of "creative breakthrough," as we find in *Wonder Boys*, when the master writer character *imagines* his troubling manuscript stack disappearing. Inevitably, these strategies—used to help viewers emotionally and intellectually identify with the characters on the screen—reduce the viewers' exposure to authentic illustrations of writers and the writing life.

Choosing Our Poison

To begin to understand how films may influence writers and writing teachers, it may help us if we look at particular films and the ways in which they construct the image of the writer for popular audiences. Consider the first important film about the writing life, *The Front Page.* This film introduced several conventions that have been used to portray the professional writer on the screen for the last seven decades. Originally a successful stage play written by Ben Hecht and Charles MacArthur, this story of a love-hate relationship between a megalomaniac editor and a distracted reporter was first adapted for the screen in 1931. Directed by Lewis Milestone, and starring Pat O'Brien and Adolphe Menjou, *The Front Page* uses ironic scenarios, witty dialogue, and gallows humor to critique big-city government as well as big-city papers. Nearly every character is a scoundrel, prone to sarcasm, cigars, and hard liquor; and the reporters in the newsroom, arguably the meanest members in this gallery of rogues, tend to use their desks more often for playing cards and trading insults than writing.

Frequently in this film, Hildy, the crime reporter played by Pat O'Brien, uses his time on the screen to size up and put down his career and his colleagues. Upon deciding to quit his job, for instance, he exclaims,

> Journalists! Peeking through keyholes. Running after fire engines. . . .Waking up people in the middle of the night to ask them what they think of Mussolini. Stealing pictures off of old ladies of their daughters who got attacked in Grove Park. . . . For what? So a million hired girls and motormen's wives can know what's going on.

Obscure as this picture may be now, according to Joseph Millichap, it's "mood of tough, seedy masculinity," connected with audiences, scoring well in the box office. More significantly, perhaps, it gained quasi-immortality by receiving an Academy Award nomination for Best Picture in 1931(56). These factors, Millichap contends, made the film very influential. In fact, it generated so many copycat newspaper movies that "the type became almost a genre during the 1930s," a genre that, to a large extent, has persisted up to the present (60).

In addition to these imitations, which codified the image of the tough, beat reporter, *The Front Page* inspired several remakes, including Howard Hawks' *His Girl Friday* (1940). In this film, the jaded reporter Hildy, now played by Rosalind Russell, wishes to leave her career behind for a new life with a new husband. Her ex-husband, played by Cary Grant, happens to be her old boss, the ruthless editor Walter Burns. Once again, in this film the depiction of the writer-who-doesn't-write materializes as Hildy and Walter spend the majority of their time on the screen arguing and trying to outsmart each other, pretending, it seems, that they are no longer in love. Although Hawks's decision to change Hildy's sex could be read as endorsement of the egalitarian workplace, Todd McCarthy argues that Hildy is

> a smart working woman torn between her professional talent and her domestic inclinations. . . . On the surface, of course, Hildy comes off as exceedingly modern, a sharp-dressed feminist before her time who can out-think, out-write, and out-talk any of her male colleagues, an unusual woman even in Hawks's world in that she long ago proved herself worthy of inclusion in the otherwise all-male group. (286)

Unfortunately, as Robin Wood has pointed out, Hildy, by the film's end, is forced into choosing between her ex-husband and her future husband—between the writing life and the domestic one—and her decision to return to the paper is not a victory, but a capitulation (cited in McCarthy 287).

The third remake of *The Front Page*, a picture directed by Billy Wilder in 1973, retains the original's title and storyline, casting Jack Lemmon as Hildy and Walter Matthau as his double-dealing boss. Incidentally, this version—much like *In a Lonely Place*, *The World According to Garp*, and *Vanilla Sky*—portrays women as angels and slices of cheesecake, as girlfriends who either serve their men or distract them. Simultaneously, the movie restores the tough veneer to the journalist character, depicting him once again as a creature who comes to life when he leaves his desk. Admittedly, this is a minor production, but it reveals the staying power of the story's scenarios and characterizations. And so does the fourth remake of the film, *Switching Channels*, which appeared in 1988. How much, we wonder, have these portraits—of tyrants and weaklings, sour pusses and cynics—colored cultural attitudes in general and students' attitudes in particular toward not only writing but also writing teachers, who, in their positions of authority (and occasional bad moods) might now and then share more than a little likeness with the films' unattractive editor figure?

More recently Hollywood has also turned its attention to the writing classroom. This seems inevitable given the movement of literary writers into the academic workforce and the rise of creative writing graduate degree programs. By allowing for the depiction of "normal people" learning the skills necessary for literary success, by emphasizing the process, and the collective involvement engendered by the workshop, these films demystify the writing process, subduing its romantic dimensions. "The teacher," explains Dale Bauer, "is the center of a vast amount of attention, and students are often attracted to, or repulsed by, the display of a teacher's power, knowledge, self" (314). Bauer also suggests that "If the culture didn't project so much onto English professors, they wouldn't have to be so systematically trivialized and parodied, on the one hand, or revered and sentimentalized, on the other hand. Contemporary movies about teaching seem to be hypothesizing the very source of this fascination" (302-03).

We find that these sorts of polarizations seem greater when the teacher is an instructor of creative arts. There is an innate tension between students seeking to emulate a master-teacher and also seeking to form a writing identity, and maturation often includes elements of transference or resistance. The process both is and is not about control, and there is often a Frankenstein element present, that of creation taking over from creator. Compositionist Robert Brooke suggests that, "The teacher, no matter how exciting a model she presents, just isn't in control of the identity the student will develop. Students are not as tractable as that—the identities they negotiate in any class are the result, to a large extent, of the identities they already have" ("Modeling" 38). If novice writers seek to measure against or up to the writers/teachers/mentors they admire, if they move into the profession of writing by seeking writers' identities, then the images of authorship and writer they are receiving are of enormous importance. These films, however, frequently misrepresent the experience they attempt to describe. For instance, in *Finding Forrester*, the master writer character appears most often in the context of home or community, rarely at the desk or table.

But even when films about writing teachers strive for authenticity—by introducing workshop discussions, pedagogical demonstrations, time at the writing table, and the like—they are guilty of magnifying some aspects of the creative process over others. Worse, they reinforce the impression of the writing community as a social snake pit, where masculine personalities overwhelm feminine ones. To a certain extent, the film *Wonder Boys*, which focuses much of its attention on the relationship between a creative writing instructor and his students, demonstrates the validity of this claim. Fulfilling popular clichés about English professors [stretching back to Hawks' *Ball of Fire* (1941) and Josef von Sternberg's *The Blue Angel* (1930)], the novelist Grady Tripp, as played by Michael Douglas, is a fop, a person whose interest in writing has developed into a self-centered obsession that impairs his professional and personal life. Grady's male protégée, a student writer named James Leer (Tobey Maguire), shapes his identity by refusing to completely accept the professor as a model, ignoring Grady's practical advice, for instance, as well as countering the elder's heterosexual prowess with a gay tryst. Yet, we suspect that Leer's refusal to mimic contributes in part to his own renewal, as a writer and a person. That is, he gains self-knowledge through the process of accepting and rejecting his, at first reluctant, mentor's suggestions. The same cannot be said for Hannah Green (Katie Holmes), a student who lives with Grady—and adores him. Like Grady's wife and his girlfriend, Hannah can't fully connect with the teacher—creatively or spiritually. (In this environment, big-shot male writers interact best with other males and rivalry and competition are the norm.) Of course we don't assume that female viewers identify solely with Hannah, they may already be reading against the movie's grain (see Winifred Wood), but they might be wise to do so actively when viewing such a conventional film representation of the writing life and writers' communities. Viewers like our student who cited this as his favorite representation of writers may be tempted to say, "It's so accurate" rather than "Why should it be this way?"

Storytelling also addresses the relationships between writing teachers and their students. In this film, however, the students and instructors have physical relationships with one another. The first section of the movie, "Fiction," narrows in on a college creative writing class, where the instructor Mr. Scott (Robert Wisdom), a parody of the workshop despot, rewards students who talk and think like him and punishes those who don't. Disturbingly, "Fiction" presents the workshop as a place occupied by angry, self-pitying wretches who enjoy shredding one another and their stories. As the actor Robert Wisdom explains, in the film's press notes, for instance,

> Mr. Scott is a Pulitzer Prize-winning writer who teaches at a second or third rate university. He is on the outside in every sense. The Pulitzer Prize doesn't open any doors for him. He is resentful, angry and bitter. And he expresses his anger by seducing his female students and destroying them in the process. There is a very S&M take that develops, but from a very cool distance. He knows exactly what he is doing and in the process, he projects the worst prejudices on his students. In a way, it is revenge.

These two films—as well as *Orange County*, a story about trying to get into a writing program—tend to portray their characters as neurotics with terrible habits and foggy ethics, who entertain the myth that writers need to experience over-the-top situations in order to generate compelling material for their writing. What happens to the identities of students, we wonder, when they watch films like these? Do they accept these scenarios as examples of cinematic realism? Do they begin to expect and prepare themselves to encounter mayhem and cruelty? Or do they, like James Leer, approach the screen depictions like diners in a cafeteria line, selecting some items and ignoring others? Or, like Hannah Green, do they accept these aspects as not only real, but permanent, and condition themselves to expect the best anyway? From our own experience—as writers whose professional positions depend on publication—we know that histrionic adventures—in the classroom and away from the desk—occur less frequently than long hours spent in research, in drafting, in working with and for readers.

In essence, mainstream movies must misrepresent the image of the writer. Certainly writers do write alone a lot, but not always. In films, they go out into the field—and this is a departure from the writer-writes-alone image. But going out into the field is only a small part of the writer's existence. And as much as we are sympathetic with Linda Brodkey's critique of the modernist scene of writing, we would not suggest substituting the scene of writing in film because films often overcome the alienation of the writer-writes-alone by encouraging audiences to identify with this equally unlikely portrait of the writer-not-writing.

Life Inside and Outside the Frame

The student of writing, eager to embark on a life in letters, will arrive in the graduate workshop, then, influenced not only by the modernist texts he has read for the previous eight years— these texts by authors such as Hemingway or Conrad or Salinger continue to shape the required canon (writer-writes-alone) in high school and in undergraduate English courses—but by writers in films such as these (writer-as-action-figure). As it dawns on developing readers that they too might like to become authors, they will match their prose against the texts they read and their lives against the lives they watch in film, perhaps even seeking out these representations as we ourselves have.

Inevitably, novice writers are encouraged not only to join their individual talents to the tradition through extensive reading and emulation but also to participate in the writing communities that surround academic writing programs. Live readings at local bars and workshops with visiting writers represent just a small portion of an identifiable process of enculturation to an entire aesthetic lifestyle that can also include haunting used bookstores in an effort to fill out one's collection of literature with the right texts and writing hours spent in coffee shops to see and be seen. In these and other predictable locales writers gain experience, collect characters, and form their own character, and always they talk about getting more "time for their writing." They learn the images and to live the image. As writers-as-action-figures on a small academic scale, they are living the life they have seen depicted in countless films, held up to them as mirrors for manners. This is true, of course, not only for images of writers but for images of teachers in general. Speaking of the same, Dale Bauer claims that "Hollywood eventually misrepresents all professions, and all vocations are ultimately sexualized" [301]. Robert Brooke throws this sort of modeling into relief when he explains

> [W]hen a student (or any writer) successfully learns something about writing by imitation, it is by imitating another *person*, and not a text or a process. Writers learn to write by imitating other writers, by trying to act like writers they respect. The forms, the processes, the texts are themselves less important as models to be imitated than the personalities, or identities, of the writers who produce them. Imitation, so the saying goes, is a form of flattery: we imitate because we respect the people we imitate, and because we want to be like them. (23)

Certainly this mix is unpredictable. There is no canon of writer movies that each writer is likely to have seen. One of us hadn't seen *Wonder Boys* until it was suggested to her by an excited writing student, and that same student had yet to view one of our influences, *His Girl Friday*. We do note, however, that every writer we asked was able to name at least one influential film image in their litany of influential print authors (and sometimes film images came more readily than a list of influential authors). It is at just this juncture that transference may begin. Again, Robert Brooke reminds us that "Students don't come into classrooms as blank slates. They come with a wealth of past experience and, by the time they reach college, a fairly well-defined sense of the kinds of persons they are. Their interaction with any attempt to model an identity for them, then, must take into account the identities they have already developed for themselves" (26).

Dale Bauer argues that images of teachers in movies help sexualize and contain teachers, and that these images (to the teachers who view them) often define what teachers are *not* while failing to define teachers as they really are (313). In a similar manner, the image of writer in film leads the writing student to fail to define herself in a way that aids her craft. Speaking of identity formation, particularly for a woman-who-writes, Katharine Haake suggests,

> There is nothing "natural" about who we are as writers. We turn out the way we are by virtue of our experience in culture, in class, in gender, in race, in family, in history, in being. There is nothing new in saying so, but when we say so to novice writers, they feel—as I once felt, so passionately—*what about ME? Myself. My expression. My being. . . .Accommodating my own 'voices' to received ideas of what 'good writing' was, I became more absence than presence.* When I learned to name the things—what I was trying to produce as well as who I felt myself to be in some relation to

those modes of production and their products—then I could hear myself speak. (191)

Instructors such as Bauer, Brooke, and Haake serve up several lessons. Students of writing arrive in post-modern graduate programs preinfluenced by a number of modernist texts and contemporary films. They come seeking to negotiate voices—the ones they hear, the ones they hope to speak with.

Writers in Graduate Programs

Images of writers in films are changing but the focus still falls on the "glamour" myth of sex and adventure—and once again dominant males sit on top of the heap (*I Love Trouble, As Good as it Gets, Big Bad Love*)—or is galvanized into dramatic nonwriting action (*Vanilla Sky, The Ring*). Of note, from our list of films, only a slight number depict writers who strive for and produce Literature with a capital L (*Iris, Kafka, Shakespeare in Love*). The normalized workshop-leading academic writer, the winner of awards and producer of a dying art form, "the book," represents a type of person who transcends normalcy, a man who is gifted with powers of thought and expression that may alienate average viewers. This possibility seems to be confirmed by the frequency of pictures in which writing is presented as a professional—often blue-collar—occupation, rather than as a higher calling. Indeed, the professional writer most often writes articles and features (*Almost Famous, All the President's Men, The Man Who Shot Liberty Valance*) rather than fiction and poetry (*Henry and June, Tom and Viv, Henry Fool*). As writing teachers, as members of graduate writing programs who do seek to compose in literary genres, where do we go from here?

Our study of films that circulate images of writers suggests that teachers and students should be alerted to their tacit and explicit influence—as we have attempted to do in this chapter. We think the limits of film roles, images, influences should be acknowledged, interrogated, and taught. In general, these images are seductive. To cause pleasure, the film must present glamorous/glamorized character images that resemble the viewer in several aspects: gender, race, occupation, education, class. That is, the screen image must be enough like the viewer to establish identification. The screen, however, must present the image in a manner that exaggerates and distorts positive aspects of the image, so that the image offered is an improved (fantastic/fantasized) version of the viewer. Presumably, pleasure results because the viewer is allowed to see the best of what she is/does and not the worst (the nonromantic real).

Inevitably, the screen image is an improved-upon "reflection" of the self. Without seeing that this is true, we are at the mercy of our culture at large. As Siegfried Kracauer suggests, "American audiences receive what Hollywood wants them to want; but in the long run public desires determine the nature of Hollywood films" (14). And Katherine Haake reinforces the problem at the more local, workshop level: "The irony is that until we can see ourselves clearly in relation to the discourse that frames us, whatever discourse that might be, we continue to reflect it back, unchallenged and unchanged" (191). We do not presume to think that this chapter and our suggestion for unteaching or teaching against images will reform the entire film industry. Far from it, since the requirements of the medium militate against the writing process ever being well-represented in film for reasons we have already laid out.

However, we do suggest that audiences' attitudes toward a profession will be influenced by film depictions of these professions and that in some sense, we have ourselves to thank, at least in part, for the circulation of available images and the views of contemporary writers as they are maintained by contemporary students of writing. The degree to which these depictions of writers will influence the ways in which writing is taught and learned are unclear, but the images we have analyzed are certainly part of the mix. The writing classroom is thus, by means of film, complicit in an imposition of dominant social codes. If we seek to change that expression we must begin with a pedagogy that interrogates received images. "[T]he success of curriculum reform movements initiated in the field of composition will depend on disrupting the scene of writing through acts of the imagination that revise the scene to accommodate our students and ourselves" (397) argues Linda Brodkey, and we would extend that argument to the curriculum of graduate writing workshops.

Recent depictions such as those found in *Storytelling*, *Wonderboys*, and *Orange County* are still limiting. As long as the mentor in film partakes of the qualities we've discussed, contemporary depictions of the workshop will still be mirroring the old values. To unteach and interrogate these images is not to purge them—for they do reflect certain realities—but to broaden them. Neither do we want to insult our reader/viewer and assume each buys into these images without reflection and resistance. We can learn from women viewers who have long had to resist mainstream cinematic values. In studying the responses of her students to film images, Winifred Wood notes

> Other feminists would argue that there are other forms of non-passive participation available for this woman [as critical spectator]: reading against the grain, for example (Basinger), or humorous reappropriation of dominant cultural messages (Rich). "There is a lot that we don't know about the audiences of the past," acknowledges Jenine Basinger. But: "What we do know is that women did not surrender their brains, or their prior experiences, when they entered a movie theater. Rather, they used them both to understand and to respond to what was on the screen. . . ." (289)

That is, we realize writers (especially women who write) do not surrender their brains and prior experiences when they enter movie theaters or writing workshops. Nevertheless, they might benefit from the support of the sorts of discussions raised here. For a classroom exercise, we suggest Katharine Haake's scene of writing exercise where peers are encouraged to collaborate on new images of writers and writing spaces (188-202). We also find that watching more movies about writers has taught us to cast a more critical eye on the genre even as we continue to enjoy and study it. We now take an alternate route to the theater, asking, how we can teach against the grain, subvert these images with humor and analysis, create exercises that broaden our understandings of lifestyles and options? In doing this, we seek to balance these predominately male depictions, to counterbalance the mainstream films' tendency to reify and engender the oppressive conditions set by the status quo. We ask, as well,

> 'What are the modes of existence of this discourse? Where has it been used, how can it circulate, and who can appropriate it for himself? What are the places in it where there is room for possible subjects? Who can assume these various subject-functions?' And behind all these questions, we would hear hardly anything but the stirring of an indifference: 'What difference does it make who is speaking?' (Foucault 187)

We feel it makes a great deal of difference. To acknowledge that we are all evolving *versions* of our writer-selves is to suggest that a closer examination of how film images of writers works for and against us is inevitably in order.

Bibliography

Baltake, Joe. 2002. " 'Big Bad Love' Wastes Its One Asset–Winger." *Sacramento Bee*, March 29. www.movieclub.com/reviews/archives/02bigbadlove/baltake.html.

Barthes, Roland. 2000. "The Death of the Author." In *Modern Criticism and Theory: A Reader*. 2nd edition. David Lodge with Nigel Wood, eds. NY: Longman, pp. 146–50.

Bauer, Dale M. 1998. "Indecent Proposals: Teachers in the Movies." *College English* 60.3 (March): 301–17.

Brodkey, Linda. 1987. "Modernism and the Scene(s) of Writing." *College English* 49.4 (April): 396–418.

Brooke, Robert. 1988. "Modeling a Writer's Identity." *College Composition and Communication* 39.1 (February): 23–41.

—— 1987. "Underlife and Writing Instruction." *College Composition and Communication* 38.2 (May): 141–53.

Foucault, Michel. 2000. "What Is an Author?" *Modern Criticism and Theory: A Reader*. 2nd edition. David Lodge with Nigel Wood, eds. NY: Longman, pp. 174–87.

Haake, Katherine. 2000. *What Our Speech Disrupts: Feminism and Creative Writing Studies*. Urbana, IL: NCTE.

Kracauer, Siegfried. 1974. *From Caligari to Hitler*. Princeton, NJ: Princeton University Press.

McCarthy, Todd. 1997. *Howard Hawks.* NY: Grove.

Millichap, Joseph R. 1981. *Lewis Milestone*. Boston: Twayne.

Montagu, Ivor. 1964. *Film World*. Baltimore: Penguin.

Wood, Robin. 1981. *Howard Hawks*. London: BFI Publishing.

Wood, Winifred J. 1998. "Double Desire: Overlapping Discourses in a Film Writing Course." *College English* 60.3 (March): 278–300.

After Words

Lore and *Discipline*

Peter Vandenberg
DePaul University

In an autobiographical essay I wrote some years ago while approaching tenure, having been hired as a rhetoric and composition specialist, I described my own long encounter with the institution of creative writing and its relationship to my life in the academy by way of a reference to my senior year as an undergraduate.

> That fall, I write an ironic poem for my workshop that juxtaposes graphic and tragic world issues with the front-page preoccupation of that Sunday's *Omaha World Herald*—the Nebraska Cornhuskers. The team has barely survived an early season game, and the sophomore quarterback, Steve Taylor, is tested—as it turns out, he *can* throw. My workshop professor praises the poem in class, and encourages me to send it to the school newspaper, which I do. It is published the following week, in two different columns, rather obviously disrupting the poem's formal character. The next issue carries a letter from a philosophy professor who accuses the paper's editor of "breaking the back of Mr. Vandenberg's poem" and likens the incident to the new president's directive—some weeks earlier—to alter the bas-relief on the school's bell tower by sandblasting the testicles off some Roman horses. The philosopher declares the school hostile to the humanities. I am suddenly caught up in a war over the arts between the faculty and the Administration. It feels *so* good.
>
> Unsure of what else to do, I apply for a graduate assistantship. . .

I thought perhaps I was done with this little snippet, having used it already to mark the moment I disappeared from the world into the academy. It crosses my mind occasionally on bad days at work, when I wonder if whatever nuisance I'm facing is better described as the ultimate result of my own careless fall through a trap-door positioned under "the workshop," or a seamless seduction by a master rhetor disguised as a tenured poet. On good days, of course, I have much positive to say about my students, my paycheck, my insurance, and that poet. I recount the episode here, however, because it has been continuously called out, in one way or another, in my reading of nearly every chapter of *Can It Really Be Taught*.

The story embodies my own disorderly association with creative writing and the academy. I wanted to be a *writer*, a desire that had nearly everything to do with the approval I received as an undergraduate English major and the notion of writers and writing it framed for me, all of which underscored a romantic image inherited from an older brother. I don't recall considering a career teaching until teaching became bound up with what it meant to be a writer. My identity as *writer* authorized my role as *teacher*, and I began teaching writing by directly relating the lore I was continuing to derive from genre-specific workshops (infused with what I could remember of the five-paragraph essay). One day I took a heavy sack of oranges into my first-year writing course, tossed them out like softballs from the front, and encouraged the construction of similes, metaphors, and sensory images. My early days as a writing teacher were replete, as Donald Rumsfeld might say, with "unknown unknowns, the ones we don't know we don't know" (quoted in Seely).

A year later, for the first time as an English student, in an MA course called Teaching Writing, I was asked to read *about* writing—not literary models, or textbooks crammed with advice about constructing forms, or inspirational how-to's from "established writers." My classmates and I read and talked about essays that obligated us to think beyond our own ostensibly private relationships with an ostensibly acontextual literary pattern. We wrote about discourse, audience, collaboration, discipline, rhetoric, literacy, invention, pedagogy, *theory*. Well before defending my thesis, a collection of stories and poems, I had already submitted applications for doctoral work in rhetoric and composition. It remains true today that I have barely scratched the surface of what there is to learn about poetry and fiction, but I was already then vaguely aware of the expansiveness of writing as an object of study and the possibilities for teaching writing—newly "known unknowns" that seemed at the time unlikely to ever become known in the confines of the workshop. Some of the graduate students I teach these days in a range of nonfiction courses might well argue otherwise, but I believe I am a much better teacher of creative writing for having wandered away from the sphere of lore to encounter academic discourse.

This report is noticeably similar to Mary Ann Cain's, of course, and not unlike those of first-wave compositionists who found themselves largely incompetent in the writing classroom after being trained as literary critics. *Can It Really Be Taught* takes its place alongside the small handful of books and articles its contributors reference—examples of the principled search for identity as *teacher* that begins when creative writers recognize that "we know there are some things we do not know" (Rumsfeld quoted in Seely). I sense in my own reading of this book its significant potential to refigure the stories we will tell ourselves and our students about creative writing. I am privileged to have my own "after" words bound up with these provocative chapters, and honored to imagine them mingling with your own, in whatever way they do. I'm thinking now, briefly and conditionally, about the following concerns, which I suspect will only continue to draw attention as this emergent discourse unfolds.

It is a sad fact that when we complain about "theory," we are almost always complaining about something else—nominalizations, bald professionalism, myopia, professional turf-grabs, arrogance, elitism, and so on. We are rarely complaining about *a particular set of provisional concepts, definitions, and propositions that, by specifying relations among variables, functions to explain and predict phenomena.* Who among us is seriously willing to discredit the role of theory in shaping our understanding of our objects of study or determining whether we leave the house with an umbrella? What irritates us—even those who write and profess "theory"—is someone else who doesn't seem to share our language or location attempting to govern our understanding of "our" concepts, definitions, and propositions. *As an institutionalized practice*, the production and circulation of theory in textual form functions to empower some and disempower others. It is not theory, then, that threatens, but a particular, institutionalized *version* of theory-as-practice. Throwing the baby out with the bathwater, so to speak—rejecting "theory" when one means to reject the authority of a particular institutional practice—tends to deny creative writing and its practitioners critical tools and a self-reflexive ethos.

While there is much of interest in discussions about the appropriateness of theory in and for creative writing, when such discussion reifies scholarly debate and dismisses it derisively as "theory," creative writing defines itself in opposition to critical inquiry. The effort that Ritter, Vanderslice, and their contributors take up here is predicated on the notion that creative writing teachers ought no longer to limit their interests, and by extension their students' attention, to the perception that what it means to be a writer is represented by an internal struggle with the formal characteristics of a literary category. If theory foregrounds the possibilities for respecifying relations among variables, a pedagogy that discredits theory would seem to constrain learning to the two options Katherine Hakke identifies herein, imitation and resistance. In the same way that one tends to recognize one's own position as truth rather than rhetoric, one can ignore that his or her own purposive actions, whatever they are, are the enactment, the *practice*, of *theory*. Where the term *theory* functions to signify *threat*, it also tends to mask the habituated practice of theory. Many of the authors included here foreground a self-conscious engagement with theory as a way to better understand why one (or one's identity group) does what one does, and better recognize the viability of other options. When we fail to recognize, or recognize but fail to teach, that "theory" is not an enemy of creative writing—indeed, that creative writing is itself the product of theory, a particular set of concepts, definitions, and propositions—we are necessarily engaged in the production of mystery. We are inviting commitment to a state of unknowing belief. From there it is easy to understand why Michael McLanahan wants to imagine his creative writing teacher as a priest.

By definition, theory resists closure, and in so doing it raises questions. It is the productively unsettling agent called for by Mayers and Cain, the vehicle capable of carrying creative writing "beyond the familiar production of literary texts" (Hakke [manuscript cited] 3). Much of the theory that currently animates the study of creative writing pedagogy derives from rhetoric and composition, and for good reason. Creative writers continue to find themselves engaged in on-the-job training for teaching assignments beside the point of their training. And we should expect these committed individuals to creatively compose connections between interests and obligations. Perhaps the near-future theoretical work of this discourse about creative writing and teaching can be anticipated through the lens of what rhetoric and composition has come to call *postprocess theory*. The term comes not from a desire to abandon a commitment to the writing act over the finished rhetorical artifact; rather, it signifies that there is too much to consider to remain fixated on the individual writer's act of composing.

A more self-consciously critical discourse of creative writing will most certainly refuse to continue bracketing conventionally defined literary genres, instead pulling them into a theory of relation with other writing practices and decidedly *un*literary text types. It also seems likely that these relations will be understood to be as they are because the circumstances in which writing is produced have an inevitably local and material dimension. To talk of creative writing as the product and preoccupation of a generalized and dislocated "workshop" will no doubt seem to explain less and less about what we mean by *writing*. As has been the case elsewhere in English studies, creative writing will no doubt be increasingly studied as a function of the places where it is learned as well as where it is deployed; we are sure to hear much about creative writing as a *situated practice*. Signifying as it does an expanded attention beyond the individual writer's cognitive processes, postprocess theory will open creative writing to the notion of positionality, "those markers of identity—such as gender, race, class, ableness, sexual orientation, and so on—that are either physically apparent or culturally constructed at a level so basic that they impact social relations in nearly every context we occupy" (Vandenberg et al. 14).

I don't have the space to work out in any detail how that post-process theory might be used to see the work of creative writing differently, but one can easily imagine the application of contemporary genre theory to the circumstances of a given workshop. Drawing almost exclusively on the simple definition of *genre* as textual category, the discourse of creative writing typically uses the term to identify kinds of literary texts on the basis of shared formal elements—short stories have a plot, characters, setting, and so on; sonnets have a fixed number of lines and a uniform and mostly predictable rhyme and meter. New genre theory, while not entirely abandoning the categorization of texts based on shared characteristics, tends to figure a given genre as a "site of action," a recognizable response that is inextricably bound up with the genre that calls it into being and the genre or genres that it in turn stimulates.

A genre analysis of the poetry workshop, for example—informed by Anis Bawarshi's model for analyzing the first-year writing classroom—would not stop with an examination of student poems, but would also necessarily consider the syllabus, the written assignments, the margin notes and formal written comments developed by students in response to their classmates' work, and the teacher's informal and formal assessment. This complex "genre set" creates both the possibilities and limitations for interactions within the setting, as it in part determines the subjectivities that will emerge within it. As the generic function of the syllabus necessarily frames the teacher as an instantiation of institutional desires and obligations, so the student's poem—as a response to an assignment sheet—is not only a poem in the conventional sense of a literary artifact but also a reflection of intention and subjectivity *organized by* particular relations specified by the genre set. On one level this seems to tell us no more than we think we can guess on our own—that students might not choose to write a sestina on their own. On the other hand, the role of genres in helping determine social relations within situations defined by genre sets may have important implications for some of creative writing's most durable bits of lore—the possibility of finding one's own voice or expressing originality, for example, or the notion that writing cannot be taught.

If Walter Ong had it right, the state of literacy was a necessary precursor to the concept of orality. Such is the relationship between disciplinarity and lore, and the friction created by contact between these different ways of knowing (and not knowing) will generate heat. An expanding written discourse about the teaching of creative writing will further push identity commitments into high relief, and it should not surprise anyone if the differentiation between "lorists" and disciplinarians turns out to be determined by writing itself. Lore, after all, is the product of material circumstance; it "is difficult to capture in essays, textbooks, or instructor's manuals" (*Lore*). Published theory, on the other hand, is necessarily distant and obligatorily generalizable. The scope of the latter encourages its practitioners to imagine it privileged over the former. While lore circulates informally, imperfectly, and often without record, scholarly ways of knowing are isomorphic with their modes of dissemination—books, articles, conference proceedings—and the written record becomes coterminous with the collective we recognize as a "field" or "discipline." Disciplinarity carries the weight of *literacy* with it, and this should leave us cautiously protective of the circumstances from which lore emerges and healthily skeptical about the formations that academic literate practices compose.

As the number of graduating creative writers increases, so does the number of creative writing programs; graduates go on to stimulate demand for more creative writing students, more creative writing programs, and more creative writing teachers. Meanwhile, as James Sosnoski argues about the *academic* reward structure, the method for determining expertise in creative writing ensures that the majority cannot achieve distinction. With too few Pulitzer winners available to staff every program, and too many schools unable

to compete for Cain's Famous Author, the notion that extensive creative publications and awards will remain a uniform standard for teaching creative writing is impossible to sustain. That many new creative writing teachers will land
in institutions where they are expected to teach a broad range of courses
beyond the genre-based workshop is predictable. That so many of them look
for help doing what they were not trained to do is a credit to the institutions
that hire them. That many of them find published pedagogical theory of value
in meeting these other demands is likely—we are conditioned to find answers
in books. And that some of these individuals are now finding opportunities
through the academic reward structure to better match their desire to publish
with the exigencies of their particular jobs is inevitable.

I cast the state of affairs this way not to promote the idea that those who
publish about teaching are incapable of publishing stories and poems, but to
foreground a range of issues that will define publication *about* creative writing
as this emergent discourse evolves. As we all move forward, we ought not
grow comfortable with a too-easy opposition of lorist and disciplinarian. This
is an exciting time to teach and write *about* creative writing, a conclusion
made possible by the rich interplay of lore and scholarship self-evident in this
welcome collection of essays.

Bibliography

Bawarshi, Anis. 2003. *Genre and the Invention of the Writer.* Logan: Utah State Uni-
    versity Press.

Ong, Walter. 2002. *Literacy and Orality.* 2nd edition. New York: Routledge.

Seely, Hart. 2003. "The Poetry of D. H. Rumsfeld." *Slate* (posted April 2). http://
    www.slate.com/id/2081042/

Sosnoski, James J. 1994. *Token Professionals and Master Critics: A Critique of Ortho-
    doxy in Literary Studies.* Albany: SUNY Press.

Vandenberg, Peter. 2004. "Auto/graphing: Wheels, Writing, and Work." *Writing on the
    Edge* 14.2 (Spring): 53–70.

Vandenberg, Peter, Sue Hum, and Jennifer Clary-Lemon. 2006. *Relations, Locations,
    Positions: Composition Theory for Writing Teachers.* Urbana: NCTE.

"What is Lore?" 2006. *Lore: An e-Journal for Teachers of Writing.* Retrieved 10/31/06
    from http://www.bedfordstmartins.com/lore/intro/content.htm?wil01

Appendix: Some Movies About/Around Writers

A River Runs Through It
Absence of Malice
Ace in the Hole
Adaptation
Agatha
All About Eve
All the President's Men
All the King's Men
Almost Famous
American Movie
Angel at My Table
Arsenic and Old Lace
As Good as It Gets
Author! Author!
Bad and the Beautiful, The
Barfly
Barton Fink
Basic Instinct
Basketball Diaries, The
Battle of Anzio, The
Becoming Collette
Best Seller
Beyond a Reasonable Doubt
Big Bad Love
Big Knife, The
Big Red One, The
Blood of a Poet, The
Blood on the Sun
Blue Gardenia, The
Bride of Frankenstein
Bullets Over Broadway
Call Northside 777
Carrington
Celebrity
Chasing Amy
Citizen Kane
Communion
Cross Creek
Croupier
Crumb
Dash & Lil
Deathtrap
Deconstructing Harry
Dial M for Murder
Doctor Zhivago
Ed Wood
F for Fake
Fear and Loathing in Las Vegas

Finding Forrester
Forbidden Passion
The Front Page ('31,'74)
Hammett
Hans Christian Andersen
Heartbeat
Henry and June
Henry Fool
Her Alibi
His Girl Friday
Horse's Mouth, The
Hotel New Hampshire
Hours, The
How to Kill Your Neighbor's
    Dog
Hush. . . . Hush Sweet
    Charlotte
I Love Trouble
Il Postino
In a Lonely Place
In Love and War
Interiors
Iris
Jewel of the Nile, The
Joe Gould's Secret
Judy Berlin
Jules et Jim
Julia
Kafka
L.A. Confidential
Laura
Legend of Lylah Clare, The
Le Mepris/Contempt
Life of Emile Zola, The
Little Women
Lola
Lost Weekend, The
Love Streams
Majestic, The
Man Who Shot Liberty
    Valance, The
Misery
Mishima
Mrs. Parker and the
    Vicious Circle
Muse, The
My Left Foot
Naked Lunch

One True Thing
Orange County
Out of Africa
Paper Lion
Peggy Sue Got Married
Permanent Midnight
Philadelphia Story, The
Player, The
Portrait of the Artist as a
    Young Man
Prick Up Your Ears
Quills
Reds
RKO281—The Battle Over
    Citizen Kane
Romancing the Stone
Scandal Sheet
Shadowlands
Shakespeare in Love
Shining, The
Shock Corridor
Singing Detective, The
Snows of Kilimanjaro, The
Spectre of the Rose
State and Main
Storytelling
Sun Also Rises, The
Sunset Boulevard
Sweet Smell of Success
Third Man, The
Tom & Viv
Total Eclipse
Tropic of Cancer
True Crime
Under the Volcano
Unforgiven
Vanilla Sky
Where the Buffalo Roam
While the City Sleeps
Whole Wide World, The
Wild in the Country
Wilde
Wit
Woman of the Year
Wonder Boys
World According to Garp,
    The
Young and Innocent

Contributors

After graduating from the University of Maryland in 1992 with a degree in English Language and Literature, **Stephen B. Armstrong** spent several years outside the academy, working variously as a chef, a process server, and a freelance journalist. His writing has appeared in dozens of publications, including *Film Score Monthly*, *American Writing* and *Film Noir Reader*. Armstrong recently received a Ph.D. in Creative Writing from Florida State University.

Former Kellogg W. Hunt Professor of English, leader in English Studies, and mentor to dozens of students and colleagues, **Wendy Bishop** taught writing at Florida State University. She was the author or editor of over twenty books including *Ethnographic Writing Research; Teaching Lives: Essays and Stories; Thirteen Ways of Looking for a Poem; The Subject Is Writing; Released into Language;* and *In Praise of Pedagogy: Poems and Flash Fiction on Teaching*, and three poetry chapbooks.

Patrick Bizzaro is a poet and critic who currently serves as Director of University Writing Programs and Professor of English at East Carolina University. He has published eight books and chapbooks of poetry and won a variety of awards for his poems. He is the editor of *Dream Garden: The Poetic Vision of Fred Chappell* (LSU 1997) and *More Lights Than One: On the Fiction of Fred Chappell* (LSU 2004). He wrote *Responding to Student Poems: Applications of Critical Theory* (NCTE 1993) and several textbooks, including *The Harcourt Brace Guide to Writing in the Disciplines*. In 2002, he was selected as a North Carolina Board of Governor's Distinguished Professor for Teaching and in 1999 as an East Carolina University Scholar-Teacher Award winner.

Mary Ann Cain is Professor of English at Indiana University Purdue University Fort Wayne, where she teaches classes in fiction, creative nonfiction, composition and rhetorical theory and pedagogy and women's studies. Her book, *Revisioning Writer's Talk: Gender and Culture in Acts of Composing* (SUNY 1995), explores the role of talk in creative writing workshops. She has published stories, poems, and essays in many literary journals, including *North American Review*, *Under the Sun*, and *First Intensity*.

Michelle Cross is a doctoral student in English literature at the State University of New York at Buffalo. She has published articles in *Saturday Night* and *broken pencil* magazines and her poetry has appeared in various literary journals, chapbooks, and websites.

Katherine Haake's fiction includes the collections *No Reason on Earth* and *The Height and Depth of Everything*. Her stories have appeared widely in such literary magazines as the *Iowa Review, Michigan Quarterly Review, Mississippi Review*, the *Minnesota Review,* and *Quarterly West*. She published *What Our Speech Disrupts: Feminism and Creative Writing Studies* in 1999 and coauthored a creative writing textbook with Wendy Bishop and Hans Ostrum titled *Metro: Journeys in Writing Creatively*. A professor of English at California State University Northridge, she is also on the faculty of the low-residency MFA Creative Writing Program at Antioch, LA, and of a new consortium-based Creative Writing MFA collaboratively offered by five separate California state universities. She lives in Los Angeles with her husband and two sons.

Eloise Klein Healy, founding chair of the MFA in Creative Writing at Antioch University, Los Angeles, received an MFA in Creative Writing from Vermont College. She is the author of five books of poetry and a chapbook. *Passing*, published by Red Hen Press, was a finalist for the Lambda Literary Award in Poetry. *Artemis in Echo Park* (Firebrand) was also a Lambda Book Award Finalist. Her work was awarded the Grand Prize of the Los Angeles Poetry Festival and has been honored with a grant from the California Arts Council. She has received several Pushcart Prize nominations and has been Artist-in-Residence at Dorland Colony and the MacDowell Arts Colony.

Anna Leahy teaches at North Central College in Naperville, Illinois and is the editor of *Power and Identity in the Creative Writing Classroom: The Authority Project*, the first in the New Writing Viewpoints Series from Multilingual Matters. She has also served as coordinator of the Pedagogy Steering Committee for the Associated Writing Programs. Her poetry chapbook, *Hagioscope,* was published in 2000 and she is the author of *The Insect Workbook*, a children's book. Her poetry has appeared in *Alaska Quarterly Review*, *Crab Orchard Review*, *The Journal*, *Phoebe*, *Quarterly West,* and others. She holds graduate degrees from Ohio University, the University of Maryland, and Iowa State University.

Tim Mayers is Associate Professor of English at Millersville University, where he teaches composition and creative writing. He has published scholarly work in *Computers and Composition*, *College Composition and Communication,* and *JAC*. His poems have appeared in numerous literary journals. He recently published *(Re) Writing Craft: Composition and Creative Writing in the Twentieth and Twenty-First Centuries* with the University of Pittsburgh Press.

Mike McClanahan is a graduate of the Master of Arts Creative Writing program at East Carolina University and the MFA program at the University of North Carolina in Greensboro. He holds a BA in English and a Master's of Public Administration. He is a former journalist and served as Press Secretary for a member of the United States Congress. His creative work has appeared in *Tar River Poetry* and *Baltimore Review*.

Kelly Ritter is Associate Professor of English and First-Year Composition Program Coordinator at Southern Connecticut State University. She received her MFA from the University of Iowa and her Ph.D. from the University of Illinois at Chicago. Her essays and articles on pedagogy, writing program design, and teacher training have appeared in *College English, College Composition and Communication, Composition Studies, Pedagogy, Profession, and WPA: Writing Program Administration*. Her poetry has also appeared in several literary journals. She lives in Connecticut with her husband and daughter.

David Starkey teaches creative writing at Antioch University, Santa Barbara, and Los Angeles City College. He is the author of a textbook, *Poetry Writing: Theme and Variations*, co-author (with Wendy Bishop) of *Keywords in Creative Writing*, editor of *Teaching Writing Creatively* and *Genre By Example: Writing What We Teach*, and co-editor (with Richard Guzman) of *Smokestacks and Skyscrapers: An Anthology of Chicago Writing* and (with Wendy Bishop) *In Praise of Pedagogy*. More than three hundred of his poems have appeared in English language journals around the world. He has published several collections of poems with small presses, including *Fear of Everything* (Palanquin Press) and *David Starkey's Greatest Hits* (Pudding House).

Priscila Uppal is a Canadian poet and novelist who is published nationally and internationally and whose work has been translated into other languages. Her titles include The *Divine Economy of Salvation* (a novel) and *Pretending to Die* (poetry). She is an Assistant Professor in the Humanities Division of York University, Toronto.

Peter Vandenberg is Professor of English and Director of the MA in New Media Studies at DePaul University, where he teaches courses in composition theory and the rhetoric of design. Professor Vandenberg is co-editor of *Relations, Locations, Positions* (NCTE, 2006) and *Keywords in Composition Studies* (Boynton/Cook, 1996). His recent publications include essays in *College English, JAC, New Writing, Reflections*, and *Writing on the Edge*.

Stephanie Vanderslice is Associate Professor of Writing at the University of Central Arkansas, and has an MFA from George Mason University and a Ph.D. from the University of Louisiana at Lafayette. She has published fiction and essays in the *American Literary Review, So to Speak: A Feminist Journal of Language and Art, Writing-On-the-Edge, Other Mothering, Profession, New Writing, Teaching Creative Writing* (Continuum), *Power and Identity in the Creative Writing Classroom: The Authority Project* (Multilingual Matters), *The Creative Writing Handbook* (Edinburgh University Press), and many others. She is also on the editorial board of *New Writing: an International Journal of Creative Writing Theory and Pedagogy*. She lives in Conway, Arkansas, with her husband and two sons.